THE LAND OF A MILLION ELEPHANTS

Written by Asa Baber
and
Illustrated by David M. Luebke

First published in the USA in 1970 (William Morrow).
Serialized in *Playboy* (February, March, April 1970)
Burning Cities Press, first printing 1992

Published by Burning Cities Press
Distributed in cooperation with Vietnam Generation, Inc.
2921 Terrace Drive, Chevy Chase, Maryland 20815

ISBN: 0-9628524-2-2

This book was produced on a MacIntosh IIcx computer with 8 mgs of RAM, a 105mg Quantum internal hard drive, a Syquest 44mg removable cartridge drive, and a Radius 19" grey-scale monitor. Line art was scanned on an Apple 8.5"x14" flatbed scanner. Camera-ready copy was printed by an Apple LaserWriter II NTX on Strathmore Legacy paper. Software used in production ran under System 6.05 and included Microsoft Word 4.0, PageMaker 4.0, and Adobe Photoshop 1.07. Typefonts are Clearface 12p normal and bold, Paint Brush, and Italic Optima Oblique 11pt normal and bold. Offset printing and binding was done by BookMasters, Inc. of Mansfield, OH.

To the memory of Mike and Wallie, and to the future of Jim & Brendan & Gardner & Suzanne & Sherri

The Great Panjandrum Himself

So she went into the garden

to cut a cabbage leaf

to make an apple-pie;

and at the same time

a great she-bear, coming down the street

pops its head into the shop.

What! No soap?

So he died

and she very imprudently married the Barber:

and there were present

the Picininnies

and the Joblillies

and the Garyulies

and the great Panjandrum himself

with the little round button at the top

and they all fell to playing the game

of catch-as-catch-can,

till the gunpowder ran out at the heels of their boots.

Samuel Foote

Try this: a jungle dawn, see? The night sky dying and the monkeys calling. The birds get ready for heat. Smoke, river mists, low clouds on the hills. The charcoal porters walk the trails. Out of the brush comes Buon Kong riding his elephant. Tall grass falls under the slow shifting weight. *Dadumdada* you expect to hear trumpeted. Into the circle he rides, beast kneels, dismounted is Buon Kong. Not a word. He waits.

A tall girl has bathed in the stream. She comes back up the hill with her hair dripping. She is naked to the waist and the water oils her skin. She faces the rising sun and combs her hair with an elephant comb and her face has the look of seeing nothing.

The ritual of a new day begins. The girl kneels and raises her hands to the sky. Buon Kong reaches up. On each wrist he ties a string. Each string has thirty-two knots in it for the thirty-two parts of the body and the thirty-two souls. He leads the group, saying: "Come, my soul, by the path that has just been opened, by the track that has just been cleared. Come with me and bouleversez. Take your tie and hang your ghost. Come, before it's too late."

Then the girl makes pipes for them and they drink rice wine. Rice wine is called *phoum.*

Descriptions:

the mountain people of Chanda build their houses on stilts   the roofs are made of straw and the walls are supported by saplings

their ponies are shaggy and small   they carry more than their weight

the hunters wear silver collars and anklets   these they may not keep if they fail to track wounded game or kill more than they need to eat or use any of the foreigners' weapons from the crates in storage

the best cure for dysentery is to chew raw opium   it tastes like licorice and you can bite into it like chewing tobacco

the people live long lives doctored by the gall of bear and python, marrow of tiger, deer's soft horn they eat onions when it rains

colors of poppies: red, blue, white, mauve   pale-green stems   collect the sap, wrap it in banana leaves, shape it into brown blocks   the women do this work singing quietly in the fields the plants are waist-high   the women work early in the morning before the dew lifts, before the clouds pass

the blues of their cotton wraps are the color of deep water on a clear day when the sky gives tones to everything

on some mornings there is a rainbow over the poppy fields   this the pinnacle of the world's prism

if the valley harvest is poor the mountain people must guard their own fields from the lowlanders

the men carry handmade rifles without stocks or sights   the bullets are made out of rusty nails, the powder out of charcoal and saltpeter   the men wear coils of lighted torchwood around their wrists

This is the story of how The Crew got together and what they did. Credit to you if you stay with it. Once you've read it, you might even decide to come over to Chanda yourself. In which case, come.

The history of Chanda is happy and sad.

When the great god Khang came out of the sky and chose his living place many thousands of years ago, he settled in what was to become Chanda. Khang loved the trees and rivers and hills. He mated with a sea serpent and they had four sons. Three of the sons were okay guys. The fourth was a real shit. His name was Yak. He was short and ugly and his mother dressed him funny.

For ten or twelve centuries everything went pretty well. Khang had his way when he wanted it. He ruled the world. The boys played together in the great outdoors while their mother baked papaya trees and buffalos for fancy dinners.

Then one day, Yak killed his father. He did it very sneakily by the light of a new moon. No one saw him do it. He simply came home and announced that from that day forward *he* was the grandest god in the jungle. Since the other three sons were spiritual innocents, and since the mother was too old by now to fight it, Yak had his victory.

Yak was a bad king. He loved to fight and he started wars and other conflagrations for his own amusement.

It is Buon Kong's opinion that Yak still lives (that is, his *phi* does) in the hearts of many people today.

It is Roger Blake's opinion that there is no such thing as a *phi*. This is why Roger Blake left his parish and came to Chanda. He wanted to destroy ignorant superstitions.

Buon Kong teaches that there are three harmonies in the world: water harmony, the harmony of living beings, and the harmony of flower-like girls. According to him, the last harmony is the best. The way he sees it, water can storm in a minute and living beings can fight in seconds, but it takes years for a *phousao* to grow old.

The King of Chanda is five feet two. In the years before Chanda became important, he used to ride to work down the Royal Road seated on his elephant. He would smile at all his subjects and they would rise up from their bent-back postures in the rice fields and wave at him.

"How nice," he used to say, "that I am the one King everyone stops bowing for."

The great Powers were afraid that the King would be assassinated riding high in profile like that. "It is not fitting, King, that you have no limousine," they said, one at a time. "It is beneath your dignity to ride in the open on an elephant."

They showered him with automobiles and the King rode to work in a different car on each day of the week. But the climate of Chanda, the dirt and red mud and monsoons, made it difficult to keep the cars running. The Americans and Russians imported teams of mechanics to service their limousines. Spare parts were hauled upriver and stacked on the docks and in the huts.

"Please," said the King one day to Colonel Kelly, the American adviser, "please permit me kindly to return to my elephants."

"No can do, King Six," said Kelly through his cigar. "Will inquire via telex but suspect, I say again suspect no joy." Colonel Kelly was very busy and he talked in radio procedure on occasion to save time.

"Roger," said the King, who was learning.

"Out," said Kelly.

The good Colonel sent an inquiry by radio telephone to Saigon. It was relayed to the Fleet Monitoring Station in the China Sea, and from there on to CincPacSix in Honolulu by satellite transmission, where it was decoded and recoded and telegraphed under the seas and across the mountains to Washington. There it was picked up by the agencies concerned (and also by other agencies who had to know what those agencies were up to) and it was scheduled for discussion on many agendas.

This is not to imply that the quiet Colonel was just sitting around while he waited for the answer. As a matter of fact, he forgot the message entirely, for he was a very busy Colonel, and what between flying chopper missions to drop arms, and establishing liaison with mountain tribes, and cutting a little opium on the side, he hardly had time to think. So it is not surprising, and certainly not to his discredit, to realize that when a response finally did come in a slightly garbled form, the Colonel did not understand what it was all about.

The kind Colonel requested an audience with the King (that is, he walked into the next room where the King was reading *The New York Times*). "You got any elves here?" he asked.

"I beg your pardon?" said the King, who had been abroad to Paris and to London.

"I say again, you got any elves in this country?"

"Hmm," purred the King as he read stock quotations and pretended to think hard about the question, "it could just possibly be that we do, although I have never seen any myself, at least not that I can remember."

These continual qualifications were a bother to the efficient Colonel. He tossed the action message in the King's lap. "Says here we got no elves' pants. You ask for elves' pants?"

"I don't know," murmured the King again as he looked at the Colonel through his gold-rimmed glasses. "Are elves' pants expensive?"

"Beats the hell out of me, King Six. I can't see how they would be, though. Elves are supposed to be small. Not much material needed. Although there's the workmanship involved."

"Ah yes," said the King.

"Yep," puffed the Colonel, now interested in the subject. "Tiny little sewing job, I guess. Mighty small crotch, I guess." He smoked in silent contemplation. "Well, I can get you a reconfirm on this, but I don't think they got any elves' pants available."

"That," said the King without emotion of any kind, "is too bad."

The Colonel had turned to go, but hearing a tone of neutrality in the King's voice, he wheeled back. He slammed his fist on the desk like a sincere car salesman. "Listen here, King old buddy, we're going to get you those elves' pants if it's the last thing we do."

"That would be very nice indeed," said the King as he read the message in his lap: NO SAY AGAIN NO ELVES PANTS.

It was months before the Colonel figured out what the message meant. By then the King had displeased many governments by some of his actions, and suggestions were made that perhaps it was time for the King to get back on top of his elephant, but the King only smiled.

"Laws do not automatically make people better," said Buon Kong. "For people must attain a state of inner truth."

"And what is truth?" he was asked.

Buon Kong smoked on his pipe for a moment before answering. "I will tell you a story about truth," he finally said. "Once our King decided that he would make his people in Chanda honest and truthful. One day while we were out in the fields, he built a gallows in front of the Royal Gate. When we returned from our work at dusk, there was the Captain of the Royal Guard stationed with his troops by the gallows.

"'What is this?' we all asked.

"'Everyone will be questioned before he enters the city,' said the Captain. 'If he tells the truth, he will be allowed to enter. If he lies, he will be hanged.'

"We stood there and talked to each other, wondering what to do. Finally, I stepped forward.

"'Where are you going?' asked the Captain.

"'I did not stop but answered as I walked, 'I am on my way to be hanged.'

"He caught up with me. 'I don't believe you.'

"'Very well,' I said, 'if I have told a lie, then hang me.'

"I brushed past the gallows. He put his hand on my shoulder. We were nearing the Gate. 'If I hang you for lying,' he spluttered, 'I will make what you have said come true.'

"I went under the arch and the people cheered and followed me. 'Exactly,' I said to the Captain, 'and now you know what truth is to those in power. It is their truth.'

"The gallows were taken down and moved back to the prison yard where they are still used with some frequency."

"Truly, Buon Kong, I think you could be King," someone said.

Buon Kong spit betel juice. "I have never felt peaceful enough for power. Places of power are not harmonious."

"But you are one of the most peaceful men I know, surely more peaceful than the King."

"It is not my business to judge the harmony of the King. Remember that harmonies are deceptive, that a chaotic soul may have a surface as smooth as fish oil."

And with that he lay back on his pallet to sleep.

The mountain people of Chanda are called the Lo. They bury their dead high on the hills above the rubber plantations. They make tombstones out of Katafa wood. The statues are life-sized. A sort of coitus non interruptus, these carvings, catching all ancestors in the act, unified in death in frozen couplings.

"We praise their love of life. Death is merely a last accident." So says the Raja who acts as gatekeeper. "Before death, each person chooses his favorite posture. It is drawn on rice paper according to his directions, and approved again by the one about to pass on. Thus the great variety you see here."

So there it is. Over each grave a gesture of final dreams. The faces are featureless.

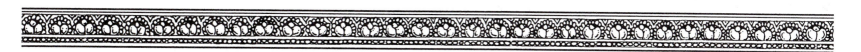

Charlie Dog came to Chanda by way of two busts in America. The first in Texas where he was sent up for having two joints rolled in his field jacket liner. The second in California. In both cases he was coming across from Mexico.

Charlie Dog loved Mexico better than any place he had ever been. But he kept getting caught doing one thing and another.

About a year after his second term began, Charlie Dog was picking tomatoes on the prison farm (under the watchful double-barrel eye of the guard) when he fell to listening to the chatter in the next field. Mexican chatter, that is, spoken by wetbacks. Enough of it was understood by Charlie Dog, oh yes. An old man of bent back sang a song about Chanda. Charlie Dog listened and translated it that night:

There is a place called Chanda
Where the women are all free
Aieeeee
And more dope than you could hope for
Unless your Daddy peddles pot
Aieeeee
So you take your caffeine
And leave me my amphetamine
Oh baby baby baby your Daddy's getting old.

There is some question as to whether Charlie Dog translated this song literally, and there might even be some question whether he heard the song at all. But so be it. There in the middle flats of California, he dreamed of Chanda and what life might be like for him there.

The next day he escaped, hopped a freight to Sacramento, broke into a laundromat change-maker, called a friend and got himself a little-diddle pot franchise, saved his silver and sold his gold, and within a year he bought a one-way ticket to Chanda.

That's how Charlie Dog made it.

"The story I am about to tell you took place several years ago," said Buon Kong, "where the National Road ends and the customs house controls the border.

"As you know, each person who passes this point is searched for contraband. There was a man who used this border-crossing frequently. He would ride up on pony-back carrying two bundles of rags. Each time the guards searched him. They found nothing, always nothing. The more often the man passed through, the more incensed the guards became, for they were sure he was a smuggler. They took to unwrapping his bundles of rags very carefully, expecting to find some treasure. As time went on they centered their frustrations on the man himself, ordering him to undress, subjecting him to indecencies that would make most men wince. But our traveller only smiled.

"'What are you carrying,' they would ask him.

"'I am a smuggler,' he always answered.

"Years later, one of the guards who had retired to Hong Kong met the man in a waterfront bar. The man was surrounded by bargirls and wore an expensive suit and was buying drinks for the house.

"'Tell me,' said the retired officer, 'now that you are out of Chanda safe and sound, what was it you were smuggling.?'

"Again, the man only smiled.

"'No, no,' said the officer, 'you do not understand. I am not working for the Kingdom any more. Please tell me what you were smuggling.'

"The man leaned back and said one word in a quiet voice.

"'I beg your pardon,' said the officer. 'Did you say diamonds?'

"'No,' the man said. 'Ponies.'"

The city of Royal City does not look like a city. There is only one paved road. It runs north-south through the center and it stops five hundred meters past either side of the Royal Gates. The city sits in a saucer of hills reminiscent of Dien Bien Phu.

"He who controls the hills controls the city." This profound thought, variously worded, appeared in the intelligence reports of the many representatives who had been sent from many countries to Chanda. This shrewd tactical concept intrigued Colonel Kelly. At night under the light of his lantern, he would place plastic overlays on his maps of Chanda, and using red and blue and green grease pencils he would launch attacks and counter-assaults, diversions and envelopments. Always, always he was left with the belief that it would be next to impossible to break out of an enemy encirclement in the hills surrounding Royal City.

With conventional weapons.

But Colonel Kelly had a special nuclear kit, and in that kit were other overlays and graphs and tables, and late at night, when the mantel in the lantern was down to a small glow, the Colonel would quietly, chucklingly open his special nuclear kit.

According to Colonel Kelly's consistent and mathematically correct computations, a nuclear air-burst at ten thousand feet of what still has to be classified kilotonnage, if delivered at what still is considered a classified point on the map, and if timed to coincide with classified temperature conditions, this air-burst would singe the hills but leave the city intact.

This made the Colonel very happy. And he stayed happy until Lieutenant Goodfellow was assigned to Chanda as the Colonel's Executive Officer.

Lieutenant Goodfellow always wanted to do the right thing. He was eager, industrious, square. He had been raised secure in the glow of educational institutions. His moral outlook could best be described as American Bland, realizing as you must that this term covers many viewpoints but could probably be said to center, speaking in analogies, as lying somewhere between the Courthouse Square and the High School Football Field.

Lieutenant Goodfellow did not think he wanted to make the military a career. But he was not sure of that.

He reminded Colonel Kelly that, in the Colonel's nightly wanderings, he had forgotten to compute wind direction and velocity.

"Atomicwise," said Lieutenant Goodfellow, "it's an ill wind that blows nobody good."

The Colonel praised the Lieutenant for his efficiency. They were both very hearty about the whole mistake.

They spoke loudly and laughed a lot. But Colonel Kelly was very relieved that he made out the Lieutenant's Fitness Reports and not vice versa.

The Colonel took it upon himself to show the Lieutenant a thing or three. First, he requisitioned more equipment via telex. The message flew through the air and bounced off satellites and whipped under oceans. From a supply shed in Maryland, across a continent by rail, across an ocean by plane, came the Colonel's request.

And one morning at dawn, when the birds were getting ready for heat, a small balloon about the size of a basketball floated up on the wind currents above Royal City. The sausage sellers and pedicab drivers and vegetable vendors watched it go and pointed it out to each other.

Stranger still was the vision of the Colonel crouched on the flat roof of the American Mission House. He was in clear sight of all the townspeople.

A rumor began that the instrument the Colonel was looking through could see into the center of the sun. A crowd gathered below the white stucco walls. Someone said the Colonel would be blind when he turned away from his task.

When the Colonel was done, he straightened up very proudly and waved to what he assumed were his followers. They waved back and went on their way.

Then an expression of pain or dismay came across the Colonel's face and he bent again to look.

The balloon was out of sight of the transit lens. And the entire theodolite had slipped and was pointing below level.

What the Colonel was looking at this time was Wampoom, the King's mistress. By fate or accident, the

transit had swung into line with her bedroom window. She was lying naked on her bed, her mosquito net pulled up and away. She was rubbing oil on her breasts. She was sprinkling grain on her legs. A peacock ate the grain.

The Colonel considered this kind of behavior disgusting and un-American and it made him watch harder.

It also made him forget the met message he was preparing. And that gave him all the more reason to set up his transit on the roof every morning and watch the balloon and then watch Wampoom.

Until the Revolution, of course, but by then it didn't matter.

It was the Colonel's conclusion after a season of tracking balloons that the winds of Chanda were shifting and variable, highly unpredictable (but still classified).

Together with Lieutenant Goodfellow, the Colonel decided that a ground zero nuclear burst would be much better.

Street scenes: midday:

by noon the markets are empty, the morning shoppers gone   the smell of fishwater and trampled mud   the air is charged with quiet   the merchants nap on their forearms   no cries now   a time after trade and thinking

a procession of bonzes passes   their saffron robes drift like sails in the breeze their begging is over for the day and their boys carry the pickings proudly   they are going back to the temple for food and rest and contemplation

dry rice grows by the roads

during the monsoon season the open sewage ditches overflow   in the dry months one finds nothing but his own waste in them

pirogues head upriver again either to fish for the next day's sale or to haul cargo to the river towns by pole and sail they go against the current   they hug the eastern bank once they pass the last warehouse

the boatmen sing to each other across rudders

nothing moves on the streets

Andreas carries a tray of drinks to the table in the patio of the Constellation Hotel. This is his night to wait on the Russian. Last night he drank with Colonel Gaillard, the French Military Attaché. Tomorrow he will prepare a curry for Major Poon, the Indian representative of the International Control Commission. But tonight he must pay favor to Nadolsky.

"Cold vodka in small thimbles for the Commissar!"

Nadolsky only grunts.

"This humble Greek toasts his Russian friend," Andreas raises his shot glass as he speaks, "knowing that had the Turks not gotten in our way, Greece and Russia would be one."

They drink, bottoms up, and the homemade liquor burns their throats. Andreas made this batch only last week. He boils water and spirits together, adds lemon peel, even filters the mess if he has time.

Nadolsky as usual is thirsty and proposes his own toast, "To Andreas of Paliokastretsa and the beautiful island of Corfu! May it one day be free from corrupt monarchy and capitalistic influence so you may go back to it a happy man."

Nadolsky still looks restless so Andreas stands again. "To Alexander Nadolsky of Odessa who has graced my poor hotel in Chanda with his presence ever since he came here on assignment from Istanbul—and who, as I understand it, was just reassigned here for another year even though he had informally requested transfer."

This catches Nadolsky by surprise. He sits stunned for a minute. Andreas smiles indulgently as if the conversation had reached a pleasant pause.

"You will tell me, of course, where you heard that," Nadolsky finally says.

Andreas raises his palms in futility. "Surely it is enough that I, a poor hotel owner, have learned of this, and that in faithfulness and trust I pass it on to my Russian friend."

"Who will reward such friendship."

"My life has been vacant of rewards, as you know, but were I to tell you my source, I am sure my life would be less valuable than a lobster's claw." To escape this interrogation, Andreas offers another toast. "To the adventurous Americans who are now flying air observation missions over the Plain of Elephants not far from our city..." He gestures as if to drink but Nadolsky wants a little more.

"... And to the newest acquisition on their staff, a Marine Master Sergeant named Campo who arrived this morning from Saigon."

Nadolsky drinks. It is enough. He rises and shakes hands. He is perspiring freely now, for he always wears wool suits. "I have asked my government to send some retsina on the next cargo plane. Unfortunately all we can offer is from the Albanians, but I understand it is delightful."

Andreas smiles again. "A Greek drinks Albanian wine in the same spirit that a Russian would drink Turkish vodka: it is a little less than gasoline, a little more than water."

"And an envelope with currency will be delivered to you later this evening."

"Ah, the question of currency is a delicate one, for of what country does the currency come? But I am not one to insult a friend, and I will wait. And while I wait, I shall remember when the French were here in force and paid me in pre-Royal *phips*. Such a waste."

Slightly high on vodka, the two men walk arm in arm to the street, past Charlie Dog, who is just sitting there minding his own business, more or less.

Buon Kong's elephant is named Babu. Once, both he and Buon Kong were members of the Royal Court, Babu as one of the Royal Stable of Elephants, Buon Kong as his keeper.

At that time, not so many years ago, the ceremonies surrounding the Court were gracious and unorganized. It was not an expensive place to be, for neither the Court nor the King had any more money than the subjects. Indeed, the King had a monopoly on one thing only, and that was the right to keep elephants, as many elephants as he wanted. Since Chanda was known as the land of a million elephants, this was no problem.

One day Babu was captured and led down from the great Plain where most of the elephants lived.

When he was first exposed to the noise of Royal City, Babu was terrified and broke from the caravan. Such was the power of this elephant, not yet grown to full stature, that he could break the rein upon him.

For an hour, Babu roamed the back streets. Once, he knocked a small hut off its stilts. He stepped through vegetable gardens. He crushed a mortar and pestle rice mill. Girls screamed and children laughed to see the Royal Keeper running in fat waddling steps through a rice paddy in pursuit of the elephant.

Just as the chase had become a very serious one, with the Keeper about to order rifles and nets, Babu took a turn through the river market. He was pelted with fruit and coconuts as he trampled produce and tables and canvas. He trumpeted while running at full speed.

Through the confusion came a short sharp whistle. Babu stopped. The market quieted. Buon Kong walked slowly down the middle of the mud street.

As far as can be told, this is what happened next.

The Royal Keeper came puffing up to Buon Kong and said that he, the Keeper, would take over. Buon Kong paid him no attention. He approached Babu and lifted one big elephant ear and whispered to the beast. Babu raised his trunk and kneeled on his front legs. Buon Kong swung aboard. Up and down the street they went with the crowd cheering.

The focus of the town was now on two unknowns. Buon Kong had appeared in Chanda only a few years previously. No one knew where he came from. He had tried to pass as a ballad singer and storyteller, and he did these things well, but most of his time was spent in the opium den by the fish market. It was said that if you wanted to hear Buon Kong tell a story, you first had to buy him a pipe. Yet here he was, critical in function to Royal City, calming a mad elephant.

"You must come down now," pleaded the Keeper as he trotted alongside the two. "He is meant for the Royal Court and I must take him there."

"If he is meant for the Court, why then so must I be meant for the Court," replied Buon Kong.

"That is not possible," said the Keeper with a deferential grin.

"Good-by," said Buon Kong as he guided the elephant towards the edge of the city.

"Wait, wait," cried the Keeper. "I will let you join my Stable on one condition."

"And what is that?"

"That you don't take over my job," the Keeper whispered with his hands clenched.

Buon Kong smiled. "My interests are few, and your job is not one of them."

And that is how Buon Kong and Babu came to be in the Royal Court for a time.

But as to what Buon Kong said to the elephant ("Or what the elephant said to him," some people have joked) no one knows. There was even a rumor circulated in the Court the next morning that before Buon Kong was able to take advantage of his first pipe for the day, he could not remember what had happened.

There was another rumor, this of the marketplace, that Babu was a *phi* of one of Buon Kong's ancestors, and that man and beast could be heard speaking at times in a strange language.

Which rumor is true, if either, no one can say.

The wet rice paddies are planted in May. There are altars in the fields dedicated to the *phi*, who could curse and blight a crop before it matures in December. The altars are made of stone and mud. Cigarettes and alcohol and food are the gifts in them. The *phi* are anything but ethereal, and our pleasures are their pleasures.

Buon Kong took the role of Chief Planter in the Court. Each season, on the first day of planting, he rode Babu to the fields. There, followed by the Court and all who wished to watch, dismounted, he rolled banana leaves into horns and stuffed them with betel. These he placed in the Royal Altar. Then he planted the first seven shoots of rice and chanted his blessing to each:

I plant the first shoot
> May you be green as the Tao

I plant the second shoot
> May you be green as the grass of the ninth month

I plant the third shoot
> May the water raise and not drown you

I plant the fourth shoot
> May you take root forever

I plant the fifth shoot
> May ninety thousand bushels of rice be mine

I plant the sixth shoot
> May I have a woman to sleep by my side

I plant the seventh shoot
> May an elephant saddled in gold be mine

Master Sergeant Danny Campo reported for duty in his Dress Blues. That was his first mistake. He left the hotel with only Andreas staring after him, but by the time he had walked the few blocks to the American Mission House, he had a crowd of children running behind him. They had never seen a man in such stiff plumage.

This is not to say that Danny Campo did not fill the bill in Marine Corps terms. Going on thirty years in that organization, he was a walking history book. Captured at Wake Island in World War II, prisoner of war who had worked on the Manchurian Railroad, veteran of the Chosin Reservoir in Korea, French interpreter for American Advisers at Dien Bien Phu, he was, on paper, ideal. And in life he was truly brave, experienced, energetic.

He tried hard to do things by the book. Thus his red-faced, dress-blued approach down the main street of Royal City.

But Danny Campo was actually a beefy, human fuckup. There was always something canted and skewed about him, either a medal pinned on improperly or insignias reversed or instructions misunderstood. It was for this reason that he was shunted out of infantry billets and led into intelligence assignments. There, it was thought, he would do less harm.

Danny Campo faced Philip Coakley, the Mission's State Department clerk. Rigid at attention, his white cover under his arm, Campo handed his orders across the desk.

Coakley took one look at the uniform and cringed. "We wear civilian clothes here. We're under the French."

"Under the French, sir?" asked Campo with some trembling. This was not a new scene in his life.

"Well, you know what I mean, for goodness sakes. That's what we say. I have no idea what the French say. Don't you have some clothes here?"

"Just one set of civvies, sir."

"If you walk around like that, they'll watch us all the time. I suppose they do anyway, but we can do something about it, can't we?" Coakley was in secret very proud that he was under almost constant surveillance. It gave him someone to dress for. Today, for example, he sported a black Italian silk suit, shiny as sealskin. He had been planning to go out for lunch just to be seen.

"If you could tell me where the PX is, sir, I'll change."

"PX?" Coakley shrieked. "There isn't one in all of Chanda, dear boy. This is a hardship post, believe me."

Campo blushed in anger to hear this Ivy League whip call him "dear boy." He judged Coakley to be thirty at the most.

"I have a tailor and I can give you his name if that's what you mean."

"That's what I mean," said Sergeant Campo. He had decided to drop all "sirs" to Coakley.

"Come along. I'll take you to him. His name is Sang Woo and he's from Hong Kong. He's a delightful little man." Coakley pinched Campo's biceps lightly. "He does marvels for all of us."

"I'd better report to my C.O. before that."

"You won't be able to see him for another hour," Coakley said with authority. "He's still on the roof."

"On the roof?"

"That's what I said. He pretends he's doing some kind of research, that Colonel. But I know what he's up to. He's a Peeping Tom, that's what he is. Come on, let's get you out of that Bellboy outfit."

It was Campo's second but not last mistake of the morning to let Coakley take him to the tailor. There he shed his uniform and donned a Cossack shirt of Irish linen, white pressed cotton slacks and sandals.

As he looked at himself in the mirrors and sipped tea prepared by Sang Woo's wife, Campo came to a new realization. He decided then and there that uniforms disfigure. He had never thought of that before. "Christ," he said to himself. "I'm thinking like a civilian!"

Major Poon spent much of his time at the airport south of the city. It was here that he had his Communications Shack. Technically, Major Poon was officer-in-charge of the airport. It did not work that way in reality because he had no staff, no planes, no power unless loaned to him by one of the Great Powers. He did have two white helicopters parked in the far corner of the field, but no one would give him the fuel necessary to run the birds, and he certainly couldn't buy it.

His job was frustrating in the extreme. He wrote reports for the UN and pleaded with all governments present in Chanda to inform him of their activities. What happened, of course, was that the attachés told him what their rivals were doing but never confessed to any specific actions of their own.

The agony of putative peace-keeping often reduced Major Poon to tears. "Why oh why did you do that?" he often cried. No answers were ever offered to this except the usual laconic, "Why don't you ask *them* what they're doing?"

The Russians landed their Ilyushins and the Americans their C-47s. The French tried to bring in Caravelles. As the tempo of takeoffs and landings increased during the months, Major Poon could only wring his hands and keep score.

One morning he was forced to watch helplessly while a Russian cargo plane unloaded howitzers manned by North Vietnamese gun crews. The Major broke from his office and ran across the tarmac.

"No guns, no guns," he cried to Tay Vinh, who was standing under his white parasol and supervising the drill.

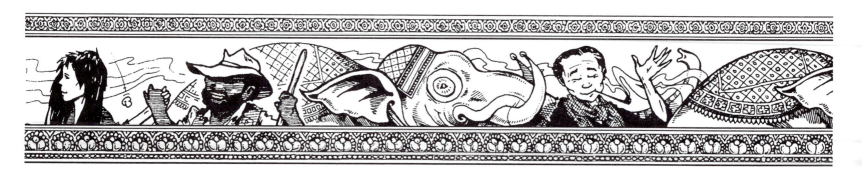

"Please Major," said the North Vietnamese Cultural Attaché, "you are in the way." Major Poon jumped to the other side of Tay Vinh. "Aiming point, aiming posts, deflection two eight hundred." Tay Vinh read from an old American Field Manual. The gun crews scurried about placing red and white stakes in the grass.

"I thought you were a writer and a poet," complained Major Poon. "Now you seem to be an artillery officer."

"The Democratic People's Republic of North Vietnam is no place for those who do not contribute to their society. You have, perhaps, read my 'Ode to the Breechblock' written on the anniversary of the birth of our leader?"

"No, I have not," said Major Poon impatiently. "I object to the presence of these guns."

"Fuse VT, time one point five," Tay Vinh commanded. He turned to the Major and smiled. "We are cutting the fuses rather short, but we want an air-burst over the river to celebrate the arrival of our guns for freedom."

The Major blushed darker brown, something akin to the color of a roasted chestnut. "I will report this to the UN immediately."

"Yes, do that, and in the meantime we are protesting the American flights over the Plain of Elephants. That place, above all others, was to be demilitarized. Why are you protecting the Americans?"

"I am not protecting anyone," the Major said.

The gunners called something to Tay Vinh and he answered. "Charge Two seems right, don't you think, Major? And do you have a place where we might burn our extra powder bags?"

"You must not fire those guns!"

But Tay Vinh had already faced about. Sandbags on the trails, crews at the ready, he raised his parasol high in the air and lowered it dramatically. *Va va voom* roared the guns. Birds scattered in the far treeline, and

almost immediately four small clouds burst low over the water, and then came the *pa dow pow* sound of the fragmentation.

Major Poon could see the townspeople running for cover in fear that the city was under attack. "Aieee," he cried, "surely you know you must not do this."

"What I know," shouted Tay Vinh in a happy rage, "is that the armed might of the Democratic People's Republic has arrived in Chanda, and we are now a force to be reckoned with." Tay Vinh led the gun crews in three cheers, hip hip hooray, the likes of which Major Poon had not heard since his school boating days on the Thames.

The trails were centered, muzzle covers attached, canvas over the breechblocks, the four trucks hitched the guns and pulled them away.

"Where are you taking them?" Major Poon demanded.

"Far from here. Do not worry."

They argued as they walked towards the main gate. They saw an air observation craft with no markings circle like a lazy crow above them. For a time they continued their argument, only half-noticing the plane dark as an olive, but then it seemed to stall and dive, and it was Tay Vinh who hit the deck first, folding his parasol as he flopped, Major Poon after him and almost on top of him, and like a mosquito in heat the OE plummeted down down whiningly down.

Only to pull up a few feet from earth and fly bottom up along the length of the runway, loop a loop and come back straight, wag its wings and dip its nose on each pass over the two prostrate debaters, who up and ran as soon as the cub-type craft was by them, and who were sent sprawling again when it had made its circle and buzzed them again.

"That must be the crazy Mennan," Major Poon yelled to Tay Vinh when the plane had landed.

Shaking the wing as he stepped on the strut, Harry Mennan hopped to the ground. He took off his cowboy hat and waved it wildly at Major Poon. "Suuueee," he hog-called, "you all haul ass over here and feed your eyes. Come on, Old Poontang. I got something here even the UN will wait for. Drop your socks and grab your cocks."

 "Her name is Dawn," Mennan said reverently, holding his had over his fly. "She don't talk, but man..."

Slowly, elegantly, Dawn stepped onto the strut. The men stared. She smiled uncertainly as Mennan reached up to help her. In the morning sun, her skin seemed basted in butter. It held the color of oranges. Iridian and prismatic she was, the best of many races. Red heavy lips and eyes that would be as hard to photograph as sand. The slightest Mongol slant to her eyelids, a pug nose, the tall body of a child.

"You can't beat that with a stick," Mennan sighed. "She's all mutt and all cunt."

"Please," protested Major Poon in an attempt to pose as protective, "you must not talk like that."

"She's more hybrid than hash."

"Please!" and the Major tried to put his arm around her shoulders, but he was a little short for that.

"It don't matter. She can't hear none of us, and there ain't nobody heard her say word one."

"Then how do you know her name?" Tay Vinh interrupted suspiciously.

"I know her name, you little Commie rat, because they told me her name. Hah!"

"Who is 'they'?" Tay Vinh pursued.

"'They,' you revolutionary punk, is the Generals who brought her over here with Special Services."

"I do not believe you. She is not an American."

"Who knows what she is, horse-fly? I sure as hell don't. They say she just walked on this plane loaded with show business folks. Walked right in and sat down there in Los Angeles and everybody thought she was part of the show. When they get over the Pacific somebody asks who the chick in the sari is and nobody knows. She hands them a card with her name on it but she don't seem to talk or hear. So you got some embarrassed bigwigs who are flying one extra body into a combat zone in Saigon.

"So I got a Priority One call to fly my ass down and pick up a passenger. They want to get her out of there fast by flying her to a neutral zone. 'Neutral, shit!' I tell them, but it don't matter, and here she is, and look at that wiggle."

"'Neutral shit' you told them?" Major Poon cried. "In those words? Oh no, there will be an inspection team from the UN up here now."

Tay Vinh spoke with a tight smile. "If this Kingdom is not neutral, it is because of white-skinned imperialists such as this one we have had to deal with this morning."

"Keep that propaganda coming, folks," said Mennan. "But just remember that you're going to have to deal with me for a long time, Baby Tay, and one of these days I'm going to take that parasol and shove it up your dialectical ass."

The girl sensed the conflict and headed for the gate in a graceful walk. The heat from the paving wrapped her figure in waves of color, and before the three men set out after her, it seemed to each of them that she was sending off vibrations meant for him alone.

Sayings of Buon Kong:

To judge an elephant you must look at its tail and tusks.
To judge a woman you must look at her mother.

Believe only with one ear.

Wars will not cease until we refuse to be vultures just because we are told we are vultures.

The wise man does not look for gold in a slopjar. Those who teach you that he does do not wish you to be wise.

The child who blindly obeys his parents is like the fish that follows the current into the net.

Eat when food is hot, dance when you can, drink enough to forget. As for my pipes, well...

The voice of the poor man is no louder than the call of a sparrow under a buffalo's foot.

If you find yourself loving your children too much, remember that you are raising snakes who must bite you to live.

The tiger is more honest than man, for the tiger's stripes are outside.

A man can find any number of drinking companions and table companions and fishing companions. He will be hard-pressed to find a death companion.

If work was the source of all property, this would be a different world.

When you are told that a policy of war is in your best interest, you should answer that when buffalos fight, it is the grass that suffers.

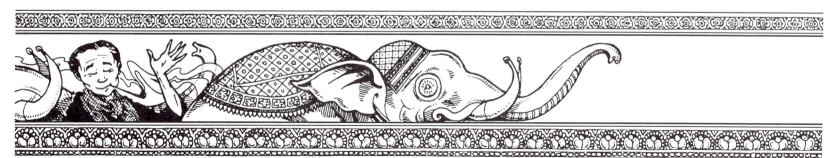

Charlie Dog was sort of spaced out when he met Roger Blake. First thing Charlie Dog saw was a white hand holding a pamphlet. There in large letters was the title *God Could Be Black!* Long arm followed long hand, long body followed long arm. Nervous and sweating in the heat, a tall blond ofay sat carefully down. Charlie Dog took another puff and assumed he was meeting either Don Drysdale or Jerry West. "What team you play for?" he asked.

"God's own best," came the eager reply, "and I want to talk to you about it."

This was enough to shake Charlie Dog a little. He blinked. "Have a drag."

The man jumped. "That's illegal!"

"Not in Chanda, Daddy. Only thing illegal here is what your head makes illegal—and then it's illegal only for you. You take this joint here. I could light it in church if I wanted to." The man gasped. "Except there ain't no churches."

"Yes, and that bothers you, doesn't it?"

Charlie Dog shook his head. "Don't bother me, man, it's just a fact."

"It bothers me terribly," said the man. "That a country as backward, as primitive as this should have no Church. A country with disease and pestilence, with superstitions, ignorant and unwashed."

"I ain't studying you, so just leave me be." I should have known, thought Charlie Dog. Another Preacher in my life.

"Give me a few moments of your time. I know you're busy. I know you're troubled. But what is a minute in the life of a man?"

"Well now—"

"—I know! Believe me, I know. My name is Roger Blake and I know."

"Well, since you know—"

"— Shake my hand. Shake my hand in faith and brotherhood!"

Charlie Dog stared carefully into his eyes. "You sure you're not tripping or something?"

"I'm on that Trip that never ends. I'm Fixed For Life. I'm on the Vision and Blood of the Lamb."

"Uh-huh," said Charlie Dog as he clipped on a roach-holder.

"And I'm looking for an assistant." This last not a ploy at all, for Roger Blake had brought three crates of Bibles with him, and unless he distributed them fairly rapidly he feared mildew.

"No thanks," puffed Charlie Dog. "I'm sort of retired here, you see?"

"Then at least read my pamphlet."

This seemed a nice out. "Oh I will, I will. Looks like you got some more."

Roger Blake hesitated, holding his briefcase in his lap. "Not really."

"What you got there?" asked Charlie Dog.

"It's nothing." Roger Blake fidgeted.

"Come on, let me see," said Charlie Dog.

Embarrassed, Roger Blake put two more pamphlets in front of Charlie Dog: *God Could Be Yellow* and *God Could Be Brown.*

Charlie Dog laughed. "You sure cover your bets, don't you?"

Roger Blake giggled a little. "Yes, sort of."

"Yes sir, you got options, you do." Charlie Dog frowned in his fog and tapped Roger Blake on the arm. "Only one thing, white knight. How'd you know whether to give me the *Black* or the *Brown* one? Huh?"

Slowly, as if he had a rat on a string, Roger Blake pulled out his light meter.

When Buon Kong travels into the countryside, he prepares himself for a long walk. In each village he is offered rice and pickle juice. Sometimes one of the villagers will try to boast of his wealth by adding fish or meat to the sauce. But Buon Kong carries a small wooden fish in his robes, and he slips that into his rice bowl before anyone can offer luxuries. That way no one appears poor.

The wooden fish soaks up the juice and is tasteful to lick as he walks.

Translated from the journal of a commercial traveller, Gerrit von Westhoff of the Netherlands, who found himself in Chanda in the year 1636:

It is not meet that these primitives should commit their horrible fornications in the streets. It must disgust the eyes of God, and it embarrasses me.

Wrapping my cape about me last evening, I wished only to stroll by moonlight down to the river. The day had been extremely difficult on my constitution, as impatience causes blackness in my nature. These people are not meant for commerce or consultation of any kind. Their simplicity and conceit overwhelm one of my breeding. They sleep during business hours. And how can I, a mere trade in stick-

lac and benzoin, how can I alert them to their iniquities? I see no way. It would profit me more to watch a spicebush grow.

But to the issue: public fornication!

Leaving Father Paul's study, I took the low path towards the village center. The bats went whizzing about my head, and for a time I used my cape as a shawl over my ears (I have heard that the bats of Chanda suck blood at a great rate; two of them can dry up the fluids of a buffalo in a night's time.)

Before I had traversed the length of six ships, I tripped upon what I assumed was a beast of many legs. Prepared as I am from travel in many lands, I fell to the side of the path and rolled under thick vines. I struck at the object with my walking-stick. I did not plan to die without a struggle, jungle beast or no.

Hardly had my blows begun to land than the apparition divided itself, split apart as if in final agony, and in my fury it took me some time to discern the outline of a distinctly human form. There, as I emerged from my wet thicket, lay a bloodied and moaning savage, his naked mate crying and shrieking over his breast.

My anger did not abate. But torches advanced up the path and prudence guided me back to the good Father Paul, where I demanded of him what kind of place this was in which the earth's floor was used as a brothel.

What I write now strikes me as impossible. Father Paul asked me in a most irreverent fashion if I had not ever used the fields near the Hook in similar manner.

It was then that I realized the corruption of that land had permeated even Father Paul's mighty Christian soul. There was nothing more to be said. I retired to my chamber for the evening and resolved

to complete all transactions as rapidly as possible (although "rapid" is a concept unknown here even to the waters).

Since leaving that place of no port, the visions of many such occasions there return to me at strange moments and I find myself ready to fall on my knees and ask God to erase the scrolls of my memory.

The attitude of my own countrymen towards my adventures astounds me. I complained to deGroot, my physician and barber, of the images that will not leave me. His eyes brightened in what I first took to be sympathy and he asked me to describe my tortures. This I did, almost daily, until it occurred to me that he was enjoying the odious pictures I was painting with words.

I told him of the fantasies I had seen, naked girls dancing with peacock feathers, lewd fornications of all sorts in the public square, women wild on jungle roots, the young King parading with a train of elephants who had their tusks wrapped in gold (a sight that would arouse the envy of our own Prince of Orange), gold and silver decorations worn by both men and women, and other titillations too gross for me to relate even to this paper on which I scratch.

DeGroot bleeds me. At times I lose my senses. My humors are not in harmony and I fear the worst. For I have carried more cargo back from Chanda than I cared to, and neither my bowels nor my brain can forget.

Back at last in my own true home, I shall sit on the canal walls and glory in the low clouds that bring us continual cool, and I shall spread thick curls of butter and cheese on my bread and thank God that I was delivered alive from that hellish jungle-time.

Buon Kong's last days at Court were not easy ones. The King was unsure of him. This indecision passed down the ranks and it became the fashion to scoff at the pretensions, the quiet lessons and hazy pompous statements that had become synonymous with the name of Buon Kong. Only Wampoon remained loyal to her little spiritual advisor, but this did not make the King any happier or more trusting of him.

As the King's displeasure grew, the teasing of Buon Kong by the Court became more open. Nothing too obvious for a time, then minor pranks of a lycée nature, the hotfoot, the vigorous slap on the back, rhetorical questions aimed at embarrassment, gestures mimicked and expressions matched (particularly the one of glazed eyes and half-smile).

Buon Kong went on about his chores in the Royal Stables and continued his discussions with anyone who would listen. His focus was upon policies and practices, deceptions and alignments. He acquired the backroom title of Foreign Secretary for the Elephants. In the midst of crises, the King would relieve tension by pretending to talk to Babu on the telephone, asking the elephant what advice his master was giving out that day.

One time, more out of boredom that anything else, the Courtiers decided to ask Buon Kong to address them as a group. Provincial Governors, Department Counsellors, Secretaries and Advisors all sat nudging each other as the doors opened and Buon Kong entered the Throne Room. He blinked to see such a crowd waiting to hear his words. He saw their smiles and watched their eyes. Here were men of power and property in the Kingdom. Some wore simple robes, others Western business suits. Some wore military uniforms.

The Appointment Secretary made a brief introduction and stood aside. The silence that followed was broken by coughs and chuckles.

Finally, Buon Kong spoke. "Oh masters of our Kingdom, do you know what I am going to tell you?"

Relieved that their ruse had succeeded, and amused that one of such simplicity could assume he was informed enough to give them advice, the group answered as a whole: "No!"

Buon Kong turned on his heel. "Until you have some idea, I cannot teach you. You are too ignorant." And he walked from the room.

Stunned silence at first, and then wild laughter at the pomposity of the declaration. The Secretary was sent out to plead with Buon Kong for his return.

When Buon Kong entered the room again he was greeted with mock applause. He neither acknowledged that nor spoke until there was silence.

"Oh mighty ones," he asked again, "do you know now what I am going to tell you?"

The ministers of state were not about to be fooled this time. "Yes!" they roared.

"In that case you may go," said Buon Kong, and he started from the room again.

The Appointment Secretary tried to save the day. He pulled on the full sleeve of Buon Kong's robe, stopping him short, and he spoke in deferential tones: "Some of us know what you are going to say, Buon Kong, but others do not."

This remark was echoed by others in the room. "Yes, very true, some of us know, but again, some of us do not."

Buon Kong stopped at the door. "Oh you potentates of power over all our lives, you who can levy taxes and send us to war and open our country to exploration and exploitation, surely you have more to do today than listen to the advice of a man who is essentially nothing more than a stable boy. Since some of you know what I was going to say, and some do not, let those who know tell those who do not." There was a murmur in the room. "Let me go back to my elephants and you to your weightier questions of policy."

And Buon Kong walked away, leaving the air filled with conflicting currents of anger and amusement.

It was not long before some of the more sincere members of that audience complained personally to the King of the treatment they had received from such a lowly and ignorant subject.

"Their complaints fell on two ears," Buon Kong likes to say now.

It was impossible for Colonel Kelly to take Kong Le seriously. The Colonel saw the little Chanda Army Captain as a crotch-scratching, betel-chewing, phlegm-spitting case of Asian Retardation. He could not decipher exactly what the Captain thought of him, but he knew that the Captain never took his orders seriously.

Their routine never changed. The Captain reported each morning, saluting and breathing garlic over the tight face of the Colonel. The surface of Kong Le's attitude was packed with enthusiasm for whatever training project the Colonel scheduled.

"Thought we'd do a little chopper work today, Captain," the Colonel might begin.

"Yes sir, The Colonel," Kong Le always answered. He talked like a closed fist.

"Sort of like what we did yesterday, remember?"

42

"Yes sir, The Colonel, just like yesterday."

Colonel Kelly pulled his Hawaiian shirt tight across his belly. "Not *just* like yesterday, Kong Le good friend, because your boys were a little slow yesterday. A little slow. That's why we're doing it again. OK?"

Kong Le seemed to think this was very funny and he gave a great Wheeee of laughter. "They piss me off, The Colonel. Slow asses! Today much better." He scratched his balls vigorously through his trouser pocket, looking steadily at the Colonel as if he could use a little help.

The Colonel tried to study his wall maps during the spasm.

"Now we're going to take the same fire teams and use the Echo One area, same place as yesterday. Good clearing for the landing zone, low grass." Kong Le thought this was terribly funny too, but the Colonel drove on. "Now your boys have to learn to jump those three or four feet to the deck when the choppers hover. Roger? Will comply? Because those choppers can't sit down."

Kong Le spoke in a believing fury. "Never sit down. Chopper must never sit down. No sir."

"And today, Captain, we'll have to kick ass if they don't hop to it. We can't have any flight near the deck for more than ten seconds."

"I kick their asses," Kong Le said as he shook with rage. "I kick and I kick and I kick." He banged his boot against the Colonel's desk.

"OK, OK, easy on the property."

"And The Colonel, if they no jump when I say, then I shoot their asses off." Kong Le pulled his .45 from his shoulder holster and waved it. "Much better today. Number One today."

Colonel Kelly sat down and held his head in his hands. The next item he wanted to bring up was delicate. "Captain—" he began, but he heard the inevitable deep rumbling and clearing of throat and lungs. Kong Le stood embarrassed, looking for a place to spit. The Colonel pushed the wastebasket across the floor. He covered his ears with cupped hands until the hacking was over.

"Captain, today your men won't bring chickens along. OK? No pots, no mangoes, no nothing. We got C Rations for noon chow. OK?"

"Maybe some bananas, OK?"

"Not OK. Nothing."

Kong Le smiled as if this was the best news he had heard that morning. "Maybe cut-up chicken and one pot?"

"Nothing!" The Colonel slammed his palms to his temples. "No transistor radios, no goats or monkeys! Nothing! You can't run a defensive perimeter like a county farm, godammit."

"I fix," Kong Le said. "Never happen."

Colonel Kelly breathed deeply. "One last thing, Captain. Attitude. Attitude. I don't understand why you can't get your boys up for this, get them pissed off, you know? Ready to kill! Just like Quantico, remember? That's why we sent you there."

Kong Le tried to click his heels but one trouser leg had become unbloused and covered the boot. "My boys very pissed off today, The Colonel. They going to kill Communists and protect happy homes. My boys good and pissed today. We fight like tigers who smell flood."

"Blood," said the Colonel. Kong Le smiled and saluted, did an About Face and left the room. His canteen was big as a coconut on his left hip, and the Colonel wondered what kind of wine the Captain was carrying that day.

Colonel Kelly drank from a mug of coffee and read *The Army Times*. The air-conditioner rattled on its chassis and occasionally the Colonel watched the slow seepage that ran down the wall. These mornings were the busiest and worst times for him. Heartburn, stomachaches, a caffeine high that was not quite high enough, another Training Schedule to fake up and file ("0900 Hours—The L Ambush; 1000 Hours—Tropical Medicine" etc., etc.), and always the vague premonition that another expert or politician or General from the States would drop in, *deus ex*, out of the skies, full of advice and suspicions.

Today the Colonel had special reason to avoid inspection. With Kong Le out of the office and presumably working, the Colonel opened Sergeant Campo's Service Record Book. He skimmed the mugshot, the statistics, the lists of service schools and medals and marksmanship scores, checked the page twelve and found it lily-white, no courts or infractions.

So where was Campo?

Colonel Kelly knew the Sergeant was in town. Coakley had told him that. This kind of incident was all the Colonel needed to make his career a bust, a nice long case of Unauthorized Absence. "That comes to about one-quarter of your command," General Grider would say. "That's like losing a Company out of a Battalion. How do you like it now?"

Oh yes, his carefully honed ass would be grass, it would. And if Campo did not show up today, the report had to go in. It was not impossible that the stupid bastard had gotten himself ambushed or kidnapped or something. Probably fell headfirst into a benjo ditch, the Colonel thought.

Nothing left to do but keep Lieutenant Goodfellow out scouting around in the quarter-ton. And file the absence in the Unit Diary if Campo did not show himself soon.

How, Kelly asked himself, how do you lose a pink and bald Marine Master Sergeant in a piss-ant town like this?

Recipes:

Cooking oil is made from peanuts or castor beans or coconuts or areca palms or bacon fat.

Trees feed the tables: banana, fig, orange, tangerine, grapefruit, lemon, paw paw, custard apple, lime, lychee, peach, avocado, walnut, almond.

Delicacies: larvae of bees, aubergines, water-lily stems, marguerites, lianas, mint, ants' eggs, stuffed frogs, catfish roe, mango cheese.

Stick-lac serves as cream coloring.

Sweetmeats are made with coconut milk and lotus-flowers and tamarind jam.

Pimientos dominate the spices, along with fennel, southernwood, ginger, galanga, curry, garlic, carambola.

Roast fish: stuff it and wrap it in the bark of the banana tree, bury it under the hot ashes of a fire. The fish cooks in its own juices. This dish is called "tiger food."

Soups are made from fish and pork, bamboo shoots, cabbages.

Rice goes with all things.

One eats quickly so that one may burp loudly. He who burps loudest may become the village leader, for he has proven that he can truly enjoy life, and he has admitted that his stomach often rules his mind.

Hilary Sumner-Clark enjoyed long luncheons in the Aubergine Restaurant. Almost always he met with Coakley and the two gossiped between courses and bitched about government service in Chanda.

Communications with Chang, the waiter, was impossible. Sumner-Clark tried to explain his order. "No no no, Chang. I want an English cut to my beef. Thin thin teeny thin slices. Understand? Thin?"

Chang smiled wildly. "You want remon srices with food?"

"No no! I want my beef sliced like lemons." Sumner-Clark watched the small back disappear into the steam of the kitchen. "Really, I suppose he'll come back with an elephant steak or something. What I'd give for a meal at Simpsons. The Aubergine, indeed."

For a time, the two drank their Scotch in silence.

Sumner-Clark was right, of course. The Aubergine was owned by Andreas. The cook was Chang's father, a little wisp of a man who claimed to have been a chef on the French Line many years ago. ("I wonder which freighter that was?" Coakley had joked when he first heard that story.) The place was pretentious enough to attract the foreign service crowd, however. There was Western liquor available, and Andreas made sure that the best of the marketplace found its way into his kitchen. The orders came out confused, food poisoning was not unknown, and

ice for drinks was unobtainable. But it did not matter; it was the only game in town. When Coakley and Sumner-Clark complained, they did so existentially, without hope of change or reward.

"Tell me something I don't know," said Sumner-Clark.

"State Secret or just anything?" Coakley replied.

"I know all your State Secrets, love."

"Oh yes, I'd forgotten. Well, there's only one thing I know that you don't. You see that tree over there? That yellow thing? It's called a shittah tree."

Sumner-Clark leaned back in his chair. "'Dear Mother, I am writing to you from under the shade of the shittah tree.'" He stopped his routine abruptly. "Do you think we'll ever get out of here?" It was their constant question. They asked it even when they did not care. "Most of the bastards in my grade are in Paris or something."

Coakley drank deeply. "No, I think this is the dead end for most of us here. A community of misfits, really. And it's going to get worse instead of better."

Sumner-Clark nodded. The food came and it wasn't right at all but they ate it anyway.

They drank Turkish coffee at the end of the meal. Sumner-Clark turned his cup upside down when he had finished. "Fortune-telling, you see? Let it dry and lift it up. Sometimes there are patterns."

They smoked in silence. The restaurant was empty now. Sumner-Clark lifted his cup and tried to discern what was in stock for him

"I can't make heads or tails out of it. You know, there are books on the subject."

"What subject?" Coakley asked idly.

"Reading coffee grounds, idiot."

"Don't be trivial."

"You say something brilliant."

A silence indicated they both had deeper thoughts. Coakley finally broke it. "The airport has been busy."

"Yes indeed it has."

"More people than usual."

"Yes," sighed Sumner-Clark. "You'd think this place was important."

"I suppose any place can be important if you want to make it so."

"Well, not Chanda, for God's sake."

Coakley smiled without meaning it. "You're thinking what I'm thinking, aren't you? You know it's not our business to think that. We're only reporters of a sort."

"Tell me, oh muse, what am I thinking?"

"I'll tell you. You'll run right home and put it into a report but I'll tell you anyway. And you can mention my name to the M1 Group."

"I wouldn't," said Sumner-Clark.

"You would and you will. You're thinking that if we're not all careful as mice we could start a very big war here."

Sumner-Clark laughed tightly. "You're almost right. What I'm really thinking is that the end of the world might begin here. Now isn't that a silly thought for someone of my training?"

General Grider sits in the warm Virginia sun and all of spring comes up somewhere in his scrotum. It is seed-time and new time. Here on this hill, he is king of all he surveys; in a sense he owns the territory. But he has been uneasy since dawn. There are going to be folks judging him, barracuda folks like the Senator and the chiefs of various staffs.

The title of the show is tongue-twisting, thought up by an executive without rhythm: *Vertical Envelopment and Its Application to Guerrilla Warfare Principles.*

The scenario has been written and practiced. The troops have been on site for two weeks. They have been run through the mud and vines time and time again. Just a few nights ago, General Grider had slept peacefully. Everything, he thought then, would go smooth as a baboon's ass. But he had reckoned without the frustrations of a newly interested Congress. That body very politic had decided to send and observer in the person of the Senator.

Momentums and directions converge on poor General Grider. Spring eases his spine only so much. The pressure building at the back of his neck tells him vaguely that this is a peculiar moment in history. He hopes to Christ things shape up.

In the morning sun, the low fog curls around the hill that is to be the ultimate objective. A bunker *à la* World War II. So what? That was the window dressing, the pyrotechnic special planned for the ooos and ahhhs of civilians. There would be satchel charges galore and flamethrowers and ye olde napalm. To the military mind, that final hill is Dullsville.

But the approaches, ah yes, they are not ordinary.

Jungle palms have been planted and rice paddies programmed. It is not hard to do in Virginia. An entire village of thatched roofs and market squares has been laid out not more than a thousand meters from the VIP observation post. Underbrush has been cleared only enough to let simple minds and simpler visions watch through binoculars and rangefinders as little toy soldiers all covered in stripes pull their shiny tiger-suits through the heat.

Ambushes and counter-guerrilla games. Ingenious as some of the scenario is, the General still bridles at how basic things have to be made for the money-boys who control the final decisions. This is not like war. This is all form and play, remote beyond belief from the real thing.

When the sun hits ten o'clock high, the limousines pull up on the gravel road shoulder. Still a trace of the cool smell of Virginia Pine. Gladhands and gladthroats. Some uneasy shuffling amongst the lowly Colonels and aides. The Senator comes forward, and he is not what you would expect. No foghorn he in white suit and sombrero. Rather a squinting and average city boy.

They have dressed the Senator this day in Army Fatigues. He wears the hard helmet to impress upon him that he is close to danger. He is calm and deferential at first, but his eyes build glitter through the morning hours.

A full bird Colonel, no better than a flunkey in this crowd, explains with pointer and microphone the purposes of this demonstration. The Senator nods as if he understands all the lingo: Landing Zone, Base of Fire, Azimuths, Targets of Opportunity, Preparations, On Call Support, ETAs, H and I Fire. The words drone on, but the Senator has to pose for photographs with General Grider. Mutt and Jeff, the two appear. The Senator is hardly tall enough to spit in Grider's canteen cup. The General keeps up a line of chatter about the weather and the day.

Not a meaningful word between them.

Finally, all are seated in wooden chairs. They look out over the blue haze of the valley. The map is to their right so they can check the progress of the show. General Grider takes the mike and croons the situation, mission, execution. He raises his arm in a regal "Let the play begin" gesture and somewhere in all that brush someone has been watching him, for a mortar round explodes purple in the sky and the smoke drifts toward earth. Sounds of rifle fire, small and distinct as cap pistols, ride on the wind. "This is a live-fire problem," the General repeats, as if everyone's manhood is firmly established by that fact alone.

Squads maneuver on the far horizon. There seems to be action in every corner of the eye. Artillery opens up on the ridgeline. Air-bursts trim trees and scatter dust like a rainstorm. Close under the OP a fire team probes a minefield. They look like children in a sandbox as they crawl slowly on their bellies and poke bayonets into the dirt around them. In the village, the thatch roofs burn from white phosphorus mortar shells. A simulated ambush on a road curve is put to rout.

For the Senator's benefit, one of the Aggressors performs a sky dive that lands him right on the hill with the bigwigs, but the kid is overwhelmed by green-faced commandoes as he tries to wiggle out of his chute.

Two teams in rubber rafts row across an artificial lake and lay demolition charges in the water obstacles. On the fringes of the final objective, bangalore torpedoes are set across the rolls of concertina wire.

All seems to be going well, and the General breathes a little deeper as he talks. He sets up the final situation: more men are needed immediately to take that bunker. How can we get them? Where will they come from? The Senator frowns when he thinks about this. The General continues to build the drama, when from the horizon floats

what looks like a batch of locusts. Moving neatly now, they grow larger with a sound of powermowers beating the air. In the deep part of his head, Grider thinks something is amiss. He is not sure what. The helicopters seem early. He sneaks a look at his watch. They are. *Twamp twamp twamp* they pound on. Grider twists his neck and tries to locate his Air Controller.

Because there is supposed to be an air strike on the bunker before the choppers are in the area, and the sky space will get pretty tight if the A-4s come flipping in to drop their napalm while the Hueys hover and release their troops. That will not be pretty, no sir, and General Grider feels the shortest moment of panic before his training comes back to him and he drops the mike and reaches for the radio.

That gesture is late, however, for the jets are screaming down now. They come up silent and sneaky and are on top of you before you know it. For a Senator, some of the flyboys will scrape the deck in devil's fashion. This they do, bouncing fat napalm bombs across the bunker, leaving black smoke and jelly fire for their next pass.

It is a traffic jam, it is, and the choppers twist away like a herd of wild cattle. They break their patterns and launch out in any direction they can find. The officers on the VIP hill wince and grind their jaws and wait for what seems to be the inevitable mid-air collision.

Which never comes, they thank God, and just as they are relaxing again, and just as General Grider takes up his canned narration again, one chopper, thrown out of the problem area and caught in winds and terrain not of its own choosing, that chopper hits high tension wires and sparks itself to an explosion. It looks no larger from a distance than a little napalm dropping.

Whether the Senator sees that or not is debatable. As the bunker is satcheled and assaulted, and long after the jets have gone back to their base, the MedEvac choppers fly into the territory. It is their job to scrape up

whatever is left in the ashes and burned bushes and hot metal. Through eye signals alone the Air Controller is sent down as Investigating Officer, while on the hill a luncheon of jazzed-up K Rations is served under a speckled camouflage net.

The Senator, bland as always, nods and listens to what is said. He seems to like everyone and to have been impressed. It is Grider's conclusion that the snow job (that is what it has been; that is what it had to be) has worked and that when it came to a vote (*if* it came to a vote; indeed there was comfort in that too) the Senator would be with them.

The afternoon is spent inspecting the mock village. Pits, tunnels, booby traps, Chinese weapons, hoards of rice.

And in the early Virginia evening in an air-conditioned Officer's Club by the river, it is agreed by the officers concerned that they have just seen what the next wars will be like (they say this with sad shakes of the head) and they might as well, by God, be ready for them. For the first time that day the Senator commits himself. If he is a bit pickled, that still does not affect his judgment.

"I agree," he says.

Nadolsky was basting in his own sweat. Andreas was a fool to call him at his office in the Consulate. The lines were tapped by everyone, and Marya Pleisetskya, his secretary, had only recently been assigned from Moscow. New arrivals from Moscow were eager, sincere, and more than likely had spent a term at what was laconically called the Hydro-Electric Institute, a place known by all to be the KGB Training Center ("Where," Andreas had once joked, "they learn to attach electrics to your hydros").

Nadolsky hurried down the alley and turned into the garden at the rear of the Constellation Hotel. It was early afternoon and the heat made him pant. He stood in the striped shade of the areca palms and wiped his face with his large red handkerchief. Where was Andreas? All this secrecy, really.

"*Psssst*," Nadolsky heard. He jumped and looked for snakes. "*Psssst*," again brought him near to panic. Then he saw Andreas crouching behind a lavender bush. Nadolsky wanted to shout and scold, but Andreas was grinning like a madman and he motioned for the Russian to join him in the hide and seek. Nadolsky was too tired to oppose.

"Alexander Nadolsky, Alexander Nadolsky," Andreas repeated with fervor.

"That is the name I travel by," Nadolsky answered. "Now what is it you want to tell me? It had better be good." He could not squat any longer on his fat haunches so he fell back on his buttocks with a loud grunt.

"It is good. It is fantastic! You will not believe it."

"Andreas Papadopolous, get to the point. If it's money you want—"

"—No money! This is beyond money!"

Nadolsky laughed. "What is beyond money for you? My heart pounds! You are the only man I know who would charge admission for us to see the end of the world. And yet you say this is beyond money?"

Andreas went *tsk tsk* in disappointment. "I am about to propose a joint venture."

"Ahhh," spat Nadolsky in disgust as he tried to rise.

"It concerns a beautiful woman."

"Ahhh?" Nadolsky asked.

"Who is now bedded in my hotel."

Nadolsky brushed his palms. "No good. Too many spies and people of poor consequence."

"I think I know a way to introduce you to her."

"Never!" cried Nadolsky, full of interest.

"In case you doubt my taste, may I say that this girl reminds me in a way of Wampoom"—Nadolsky sucked in his breath—"but she is to Wampoom as one of your satellites is to the sun. She makes Wampoom look like a Sputnik with a head full of wires."

Andreas stopped talking. The two men sat motionless in the shade; a silent struggle of wills with the outcome never in doubt.

"You were saying?" Nadolsky finally surrendered.

Andreas leaned closer and whispered. "She arrived this morning. She claims she is ill. At least that is how I interpret her. I said I would bring a doctor." He paused again. "Surely you read my thoughts."

"They are filthy thoughts."

Andreas grinned. "I thought you would like them."

"I cannot pose as a doctor. Surely the girl would know we were fakes."

Andreas rubbed his hands like a miser. "Sometimes you underestimate your poor compatriot. I am giving you access to the perfect woman, and when you see what I mean you will trade one hour with her for another siege of Leningrad, such is her power."

"She will scream. She will betray us."

"That is, shall we say, the icing on the cake. For she cannot scream, she cannot talk."

"I do not understand."

"She is deaf and dumb," said Andreas.

Nadolsky jumped to his feet. "You are right! The perfect woman!"

Andreas rose and dusted the seat of his pants. "Straighten your tie, Alexander Nadolsky. A man does not meet an angel while wearing a crooked tie." He brushed lightly at Nadolsky's shoulders while they talked. "I do not know her sickness. We must proceed carefully—up to a point, if you know what I mean."

"'We?' You said 'We?' If I am the doctor, then I will decide what treatment is needed."

"And if I am the doctor's agent, I must have my percentage."

They glared at one another for a moment. Then Andreas smiled sweetly. "After all, there should be enough there for both of us. She will be silent and neutral. Why should we argue?"

With a rolling of drums in both their heads, they stepped sprightful and lively into the hotel, climbed the stairs, paused at the door to check dress and image. Andreas knocked, nothing was heard, knock again, nothing again. Enter the two rogues.

The wooden shutters were closed. Cracks of light seeped through and bounced off the ceiling. In the dim light of the chamber, Nadolsky could see an ancient four-poster decorated with dirty white damask trimming. There in the center of the huge mattress lay the spangled girl. She seemed phosphorescent, like salt water at night. Her dark hair was spread in a wide corona around her head. Nadolsky noticed nothing else, neither the cracks in the plaster nor the two lizards that crawled around the broken fan nor the dead and dangling lightbulb.

"Madam Dawn," Andreas said nervously as he touched her arm. "I have brought to you Doctor Alexander." Her eyes were shut tight. "For what ails you?" Her head turned slowly towards them and the eyelids flickered in recognition. Andreas took her hand and placed it firmly in Nadolsky's. "First the pulse?"

"Yes," said Nadolsky, deeply, "always first the pulse because the beat of the heart is like the signal of the drum." His fingers pinched and slipped about her wrist as he searched for the proper place. "Hmm, the pulse is rapid but sophisticated." Nadolsky stumbled in his excitement.

"Ah yes, sophisticated," said Andreas as he wiped her upper lip with his forefinger. He felt her ears with his two hands, rubbing them between thumb and fingers as if he was feeling sand in oil. "She has only a little fever."

Nadolsky straightened up. "I am the doctor and will decide if she has fever or not. I do not expect a hotel-owner to tell me these things."

Andreas shrugged. This was not the time to argue but to prepare.

"I am sure you will be fine, my dear, but I must make some tests, you understand?" Nadolsky patted Dawn's hand. "Some tests. Your symptoms are mild and I suspect nothing serious." As he talked he tried to explain himself in sign language. He stroked his stomach and rolled his eyes, but it did not seem to communicate to her.

The two of them, in near perfect concert, pulled her to a sitting position and unwrapped the shawl from her shoulders. She tried to twist away. Nadolsky threw the rainbow cloth across the room and grabbed her by the back of the neck. "Ah ah, my pretty, this is for your own good. I must make an exam."

Now only the material of the sari to shed. In the half-light, her shoulders looked more full, her breasts more high. Andreas tugged at the front of the sari and peeked towards her belly. She pushed herself flat against the

bed. The struggle became more open and violent. Both men issued instructions. The could only control part of her, never her middle, but this in itself was frustrating to them as she humped and pumped her hips wildly.

"She is a fighting fish," said Andreas.

"Sit on her knees," Nadolsky heard himself yelling at the top of his voice. Why was he so loud? Then he heard the helicopters overhead, a sound quite common in Chanda these days. They pounded the air above the hotel as they flew low into the airport.

"What?" Andreas asked, but his ears could contain only the thump of the skywash above him.

For a few seconds all were deaf-mutes.

And after the sound cleared the air, it still had not cleared the two men's heads and they kept shouting.

When in the door broke Harry Mennan. He had been sauntering over to check his cargo, hoping to get a little now that she was settled in the bed, when he heard the aggressions and up the stairs he roared ready for bear. With wooden splinters in his shoulders, he stared at the two startled lechers. Slowly, they released Dawn. She rolled onto her side with tears in her eyes and watched Mennan as he bow-legged deliberately across the tiles.

"Drop your meat and beat retreat, you motherfuckers," he growled.

Andreas fluttered like a crow. "Madam Dawn is ill, Harry Mennan, and she should not be disturbed."

"She couldn't be sicker than she is with you two hog-tying her, Andreas."

Nadolsky did not seem scared. "Your interest in her comfort and safety is touching. How protective you Americans can be when you want something yourselves."

"You're nothing but a dirty samovar, Nadolsky."

"If you would like a duel, we shall have a duel. But do not play Western movie star with me."

Mennan took a poke at the Russian's jaw, but Nadolsky was no chump and he countered with a hard punch to the gut. Andreas jumped on Mennan's back and the war was on. They rolled across the floor. Chairs busted and tables fell. Mennan was all knees and elbows; he fought like a cowpuncher. Nadolsky was more scientific and waited for the right moment to hit. Andreas was just plain dirty.

On the bed, the girl lay confused and frightened. She held the mosquito netting against her chest. The dust rose from the floor and she watched the motes in the light. She could not hear the grunts and thuds.

As she faced the broken door and waited for her fate, a new light fell on her back. She turned and saw the shutters swinging open. There on the ledge, a vine like a rope in his hands, perched Charlie Dog. He beckoned to her. She smiled and sat up. Gesture again; come with me. She wiped her eyes; why not? Slowly, unsteadily, she got to her feet and tiptoed to the sill. Charlie Dog laughed to see her so cautious in the midst of battle. The rickety sink in the corner had just broken and was spilling grey porcelain over the three warriors. Still they fought.

Dawn waited to be shown what to do. Charlie Dog reached around her waist. She hugged his neck and jumped lightly onto his thighs. He rose and stood full height in the window as she clung to him. He grasped the vine in both hands and pushed off into the air, slid the length and hit the deck.

"I don't know you, baby," he said into her eyes, "but I heard all them creeps talk about you, and I figure we might as well let them talk some more." He laughed and picked her up again. "Come on, sweet chicken, there are better things to do in Chanda than fight."

She laughed soundlessly and they took off running through the garden, out onto the street that led towards

the river, Charlie Dog in his faded levis and open shirt and rope-soled sandals, Dawn following, towed along on his arm like a bright falcon.

Spring in Washington, D.C. Early spring, that is, before the humidity hits and the cherry blossoms fall. Walter Glover has opened the windows of his apartment. The sounds of late traffic in Rock Creek Park come up to him. This report he is writing dominates his mind, even now. Margaret, a young chick from the Department, is not paying much attention to his chatter.

"It's crazy the way things stay in my head," he says embarrassed and almost laughing. "Like at one time, seventy-eight per cent of the Americans in Chanda were from Princeton. Seventy-eight percent!"

Neither one of them says anything for a while until astride of him she jokes, apropos of nothing in particular, "They don't teach you to pick locks at Princeton."

Silence again. Then he moans in new fatigue. "I've got to have that report ready by six this morning. I hate the early watch."

"T.S.," she says. She is Bryn Mawr, blonde and lean, bred like a racehorse, and she combats the male world she works in by assuming a tough lingo.

"Come on," Glover whines, trying to get up, "cut that out." Terrier-like, she shakes the limp noodle in her mouth. He lies back again and recites any litany by rote in an attempt to gain strength.

"'Chanda is the gateway to the rice bowl of Southeast Asia.' Everybody says that. I'm supposed to say it. I even thought of writing that Chanda was the Gateway to the Gateway of Southeast Asia. I mean you'd have a pretty hard time getting people up in arms about a gateway to a gateway. Jesus, I wish there was somebody outside to talk to about it. I tried to leak a little to Edelman, but he won't write it up. Edelman had some reason for taking us out tonight. It wasn't just to spend his editor's money, was it? No sir. He wants to go on our trip over there with General Grider. Inspection Tour Number One Hundred and Eight. When In Doubt, Inspect. I've got to get shots for that, too. Boy, I hate shots more than anything. Always have. I should have gone to law school and I wouldn't have to do all this dirty work. I'm just not cut out for it."

"Walter," Margaret scolds and raises her head.

"What what?" he asks fast.

She sighs. "What what nothing what. Jabber jabber jabber, Walter. Do you want to talk or fuck?"

Danny Campo woke up with a porcelain pillow under his neck. He thought maybe he was dead in a morgue. Come back world, he said to himself. Ho world, here world, nice world, come on back. His eyes faded into focus. Shipboard? On a Chinese junk? What the fuck, hey, around him several slopeheads lying in their bunks and sleeping or staring. Campo found himself on the bottom tier. His ass rested on plywood. His mouth tasted like crushed violets.

A classy gook girl rolled pellets in her fingers. Campo raised himself on his elbow and looked at her. She was speaking to her counterpart, an old man of yellow skin and wispy beard who sucked on his pipe as if it was sugar cane.

The girl took a pellet and held it over the flame on the end of a needle. In his fog, Campo thought perhaps she was roasting marshmallows. He signalled that he wanted one. She ignored him.

Campo lay in the bunk. Who was above him? Who was around him? His sins came back to him. I am a wild Indian, he said to himself. They will ship me out of here with my ass in a sling and my head tucked under my arm. I am over the hill in every possible way. He plucked at his crazy-quilt memory. Fragments came back to him; Sang Woo and his silk suits, drinks of smoky Scotch, rice wine—when? When? Campo rubbed his knuckles in his eyes.

A light tap sounded in his ear. The girl clicked the needle against the bamboo pipe to attract his attention. She neither smiled nor looked at him. He was holding up the works, he realized, so he took the pipe and puffed on it.

My head has been cutting out on me these last few years, Campo thought; I've got to watch that. He held the smoke in his lungs. It burned. But all around him suddenly there was the smell of earth, and he liked that. His pipe dreams were peaceful and (he thought this even while in revery) licentious.

Later, he would swear he heard the old man across from him tell a tale to the room in general: "I will tell you a story," the old man said.

"Once there was a fool who had a son by way of the village madwoman. The fool and the madwoman brought the boy up in their fashion. They taught him how to beg and steal, how to tell time by the shadows, how to visit with the *phi* and learn their pleasures. They lived in the rain forests when they could, and during the monsoons they came to town and sheltered under huts.

"One day, the fool decided that his son was not learning enough, and that unless he gave his son a formal education, the boy would be no better than his father. Without consulting the madwoman, the fool took the boy by the hand and led him to the steps of the City Lycée. It was playtime and the children of the rich folk were in

the schoolyard. Their laughter became directed at the father and son, two beggars in rags, who stood lost and confused on the steps.

"Finally, the Headmaster appeared. He gave some rice cakes to the two figures and expected them to go away. They did not, and the jeers from the children grew louder. The Headmaster asked the fool what he wanted.

"'I wish to enter my son in your school,' the fool said proudly.

"'The Headmaster smiled tolerantly. 'I am sorry,' he said, 'but anyone who wishes to go to this school must pass an exam. And there are other conditions which we won't discuss now.'

"The fool saluted the Headmaster. 'My son is ready for any exam you might wish to give him.' The schoolchildren cheered and gathered around.

"The Headmaster tried to walk back in the door of the school, but the fool grabbed the sleeve of his business suit. 'You must examine my son,' he said. 'Look at him. Is he not as tall and straight as these other children? See his smile? You must ask him some questions.'

"It had now become a public issue, for a considerable crowd had gathered. The boy grinned widely and picked at the lice in his scalp. 'Ask, ask,' the fool repeated.

"'Very well,' sighed the Headmaster. He paused to think up a supremely ridiculous question. 'What,' he finally asked, 'is an aubergine?'

"The fool watched while his son pondered. 'An aubergine is... an aubergine is... ' the boy mumbled several times.

"'Yes?' asked the Headmaster as he picked up his bell to signal the end of recess.

"'An aubergine is... a puppy which has not opened its eyes!'

"There was great laughter from the children. The Headmaster was forced to smile himself while he rang the bell loudly. The children streamed past. The school doors closed, and only the fool and his son were left in the yard. The boy still grinned.

"The fool held his son by the shoulders and looked with pride into the boy's eyes. When he spoke, however, there were tears gurgling in his throat: 'Excellent, my son, excellent. As good as your father could have done. And I never told you the answer, did I? No, my son, you learned that for yourself.'

"And the two of them walked hand in hand back into the forest."

Campo found himself laughing only a little at the story. He rolled on his side again and looked at the old man. "What happened?" Campo asked. "I mean, did he get in school?" No answer, and Campo had an afterthought. "I came out of the woods too."

The pipe drew harder. A mild ache hit Campo somewhere behind his eyes. He tried to sleep.

After a time, he felt the girl shake his shoulder. He came to consciousness alert and ready. She pointed at the door. There at the top of the stairs peeked a pale face. Campo categorized it instantly. Shit oh dear, he thought, Lieutenants are my special plague.

"Sergeant Campo?" the voice asked pseudo-tough and righteous.

"Yes sir," Campo answered in resignation, and his mind added, Do wild bears shit in the woods?

"I'm Lieutenant Goodfellow. The Colonel would like to see you. We've been looking all over for you, too."

Campo pulled in his belly as tightly as he could and walked through the dusty halls. The Lieutenant

followed. Just as they climbed into the open jeep, Campo saw a black man run past, goateed and frizzled, laughing and shouting to the shining woman he dragged along. Goodfellow spun the wheels in the red dust and lurched off. Wait a minute, wait a minute, Campo wanted to say, that's one of the finest women I ever eyeballed. But he supposed the Lieutenant would not understand, so he kept his mouth shut and sat back in the seat with his arms folded over his stomach.

His time had come. Time for the Stockade, he guessed. At my age, he thought, I won't get to that line halfway fast enough for those guards; the Brig and me, we'll see too much of each other to fool each other.

Colonel Kelly held the message at arm's length. Then he took out his cigarette lighter (battered Zippo case, one of many in history that had taken shrapnel and saved a life and been kept as a token) and lighted the corner of the paper. Held at right angles to the breeze from the air-conditioner, and it burned fast and bright. Kelly singed the tips of his fingers before he dropped the flaming ashes into the ashtray.

There, that did it, the small and impotent but nonetheless satisfying Finger to those behind the message. First and last to General Grider, who had been a burr under the saddle of Colonel Kelly's career. They had started with the same date of rank, the same basic training, the same MOS, and yet Grider had done things right, had made General, and here was Kelly, out in the boonies and unlikely ever to be privileged enough to bask in a comfortable billet by the Potomac.

Inspection Tours; bah humbug.

General Grider's visit signalled upbeat. Kelly knew that; he was no constant fool. And to get true upbeat, the situation would have to be analyzed as deteriorating. And the easiest way to do that was to label as incompetent

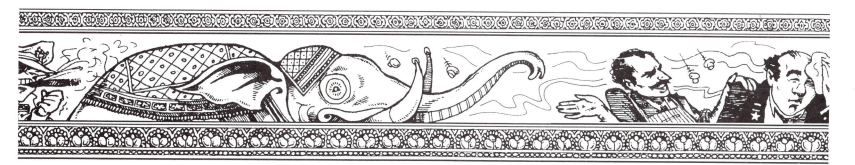

the job done so far. So the chips were down. Grider's Team was coming with its civilian adviser and agricultural expert and topographical specialist and photo interpretation officer. They would find what they had decided to find. They would talk to mirrors. It would be a time of surfaces.

It would be a holding action for Kelly. He would not receive praise, that he knew. But the point was to keep himself covered and to convince them that he had done all that he could, given the paltry means at his command.

The Colonel sat back and thought about that. What he needed was a Big Gesture that proved he knew the country and the people.

Coakley dropped in. His face was awestruck and pale as if he had just felt twinges of a coronary. "They're coming," was all he could say.

"Uh huh," Kelly sighed. "Grider and Company."

"I don't have any records. They'll want to see my files, but I don't really have any."

"Your problem," Kelly murmured.

"They're bringing that little shit Glover."

"Who?"

"Walter Glover. I was in a Foreign Service school with him once."

"Oh," said Kelly, not caring.

Coakley became more foppish in his anger. "You know, I always assumed that if they were mean enough to send us out here, the least they could do would be to leave us alone. Don't you think? You take the British—"

"—I can't take the British."

"—Hardly ever do you see Sumner-Clark flapping around the way we have to. It makes me so mad I could spit."

Colonel Kelly was only half-listening while he ran down his own inspection checklist. He kicked the wastebasket towards Coakley's feet. "So spit."

"I was using a figure of speech. You don't listen either. No one listens out here."

"That's for sure."

"Yes, that *is* for sure," Coakley whimpered with a slight whine in his throat. "You could tell them the woods were burning and they wouldn't listen to you unless it fit their theories."

"The woods will be burning soon," said Kelly in a voice of doom.

Coakley sat silent and waited for an amplification of the remark. The trouble with me is I'm always playing the reporter, he thought to himself; I don't bitch enough; I listen too much.

"Yes sir," Kelly went on because the silence invited him to, "the woods will be fucking burning."

"I hate that word," said Coakley.

"I suppose you call them 'jungles' huh? Well they are 'woods' to me."

"I meant 'fucking.' I hate the word 'fucking.'"

Colonel Kelly said in his head, Of course you do, you little queer. But he only smiled on the surface. "Sorry 'bout that."

"Why can't they just leave us alone?"

"Don't know." Kelly shook his head. "I guess they get scared if something is left alone too long."

"Do you know I've been sort of Chief of Mission for three years now? Except for visiting firemen, of course."

"So what? Same here this year for me. But things are going to change now. Grider, he come. Heap big buildup maybe."

"I don't have any files. Do you have any files?" Coakley seemed desperate.

"That's my business," gloated Kelly.

"Well," said Coakley in retaliation, "at least I haven't lost some of my people."

Kelly cringed. He had almost forgotten that for a moment.

Coakley kept the pressure on. "I hate to think what General Grider will say when he learns that one of your very own new and shining Master Sergeants has gone away. I mean, I may not have files, but you don't even have *people*!"

Coakley stood to his height and puffed his chest. Kelly held his head in his hands in despair. Frozen time, one in triumph.

When in came Lieutenant Goodfellow. "I've got him," he said in his lowest Man of Destiny voice.

Kelly jumped to his feet and yelped, "Where, where?"

"Here," Goodfellow said as he pulled the shamefaced Danny Campo past the door.

"You better get some files, Coakley," yelled the Colonel," "because I've got all my people now!"

"Hey Buon Kong," Charlie Dog said as he smoked, "tell us about them *phi*." Charlie Dog dragged the word out to a whistle—*pheeeeee*. "Because if this place is as spooked as you make it sound, I may have to leave."

Dawn made another pipe for Buon Kong as he spoke.

"The *phi* are like ghosts. They are the living-dead. They are in the trees and rocks and mountains. They are in animals and humans. No one who is harmonious should fear the *phi*."

"Uh huh," said Charlie Dog after a while, after it all sank in through the calm and happy fog. "Uh huh. That's better." He placed his hands along Dawn's jawline. "I am sure glad to hear that, because I'd hate to leave this little girl just when I was getting to know her."

"You must not be concerned," Buon Kong said to Charlie Dog, "since the *phi* regard you as the elephant regards the bamboo tuft."

"Uh huh," said Charlie Dog again, but then he rolled on his side and looked at the old man. "Wait a minute. The elephant steps on the bamboo tuft."

"Yes, and there are *phi* in your soul right now."

"That's not so good," Charlie Dog moaned.

"The bamboo tuft springs up again. It grows and lives and lets the elephant live. So it is with the *phi*. They torment only those beings and objects that threaten life."

"Hey, Buon Kong," said Charlie Dog, "that's beautiful. I mean, I don't really believe all of that, but it's beautiful anyway."

"Sometime," said Buon Kong, "you may be fortunate enough to participate in our *phoo,* our gentle time, when the *phi* come together and demand harmony of everyone."

"Yeah," said Charlie Dog with some interest, "that would be a super love-in, that *phoo* would." Feelings, vague but ever present, made him search out Dawn again. She was lying back in her bunk, sound asleep now that the pipes had been made. It had been a tough run to the river and a long hard day for her. Yes it had. But they were here now, safe as cubs in this den, and Charlie Dog decided that sleep was the next best thing for him too.

Colonel Kelly tipped the cold ash of his dead cigar into the palm of his hand. He pushed it around silently.

It looks like a rat turd, thought Campo irrelevantly. He was accustomed to thinking stupid things in times of pressure; he did this on purpose. It cooled his mind.

The Colonel was not talking about much either. He was letting the silence grow on Goodfellow. In time the Lieutenant would leave, would get the picture that Kelly wanted this fish to himself.

Finally, Goodfellow bowed out. He did not want to stay any longer in that dead space.

That left Campo standing in his bright shirt and slacks, his beer belly pulled in as far as it would go, his posture neither at attention nor parade rest, but somewhere between those formalities. The two old pros screwed up their energies and wits. Each saw his job as delicate.

Kelly set a tentative tone. "Sit down, Sergeant," he said.

Campo sat without a word. Another pause.

"Looks like you've got a problem," Kelly said.

Campo shrugged; it was a lead, anyway, Campo figured. Any man who tells you that *you* have a problem, well, that guy is trying to cover up his problems.

"Yes sir," said Kelly (and Campo thought, Aha; a man who wants to be liked!) "a U/A on your page twelve would be a sad mark at the end of a long and worthy career."

Campo thought he had it now; it seemed that there was a bargain that might be made.

Another pause. Kelly sighed. "I'm waiting to hear from you, Top."

Campo sighed too. He tried to make it sound like a compromise between repentance and boredom. "I don't know what to say, Colonel." Campo waited on that but Kelly stared him down. "I don't even know why they sent me to Chanda, Colonel." This last came out as a bit of a whine, and Campo held his tongue.

"We'll get to that. But first I have to complete my report."

Campo's stomach expanded again, in relief. There was no report to complete, really. Either Colonel Kelly had listed him as absent in the Unit Diary or he had not. Give me two minutes in your files and I'd know how to play this, Campo thought.

"Well sir," Campo began, and with some dignity he explained most of what had happened. Kelly listened tolerantly. It was no confession, this monologue, just the high points, just enough that was personal so that Kelly would know Campo was placing himself at the Colonel's mercy.

When the story was done, the Colonel made his move. "OK, Top," he said slowly, "you don't know why you're here, right? Well, let me tell you something. You're here because I asked for you." Thanks a load, Campo thought, but he tried to keep a straight face. "It just so happens that you are a very particular Marine. Do you know why? Try to guess. Try to think of something in your background that is unique and individual."

Campo's fine sense of crudities rose up in him and he wanted to say, "You've been talking with my wife."

But this was a square and serious time, he guessed—it was getting more difficult for him to judge that as he grew older—so he did not joke. "I don't know," he said. "I got the same MOS as most folks here."

The Colonel smiled like a teacher. "This doesn't have anything to do with that. Think back, way back." Campo pretended to. "Any clues?" Campo shook his head. Kelly preened himself. He loved power, and he took it any way he could get it. "Back to your boyhood days, eh, Top? What did you do then?"

"Not much I can talk about," Campo tried to joke, but it made no impression on the Colonel.

"The circus, remember? The circus?"

Maybe he's crazy, thought Campo, and then out loud he said, "Yes sir, the circus. Yes sir." He shook his head in supposed fondness for the days gone by. "How did you learn about that?"

"We have our ways," said Kelly, full of mystery and seriousness. "You worked in a circus. And what did you do?"

Why don't you tell me, Campo wanted to say, but he said, "Lots of things. Helped fold the pram tents, drove stakes, stuff like that."

"Go on."

"Well, not much else. I was just a dumb kid who ran away from the farm. They put me on any work they had for me. Then I ditched that job and joined the Corps."

"Go on."

Campo searched his brain for conversation and then gave up. "That's about it."

"You have left out one very important fact," said Kelly in irritation.

If you've got my jail record you'd better bring it out, thought Campo, because that was years ago and I don't admit to much of it.

"And that fact can be summed up in one word," said Kelly.

"Which is?" asked Campo with no pretense of respect for this game.

"Elephants," said Kelly slowly as if the word was a great delicacy that few understood. "Elephants."

There was a grim and gloating silence. Camp struggled to understand.

"You worked with elephants in the circus, didn't you?"

"Yes sir. Sometimes. I mean, I watered them and cleaned the shit out of their cages."

Kelly leaned back and chewed another cigar. "You like elephants, Sergeant Campo?"

"I never really thought about it, Colonel. They're OK, I guess."

Kelly chewed faster as he got more excited. "It's very hard to find people who have worked with elephants. I suppose you know that?"

"Yes sir," Campo agreed helplessly.

"But, I say again *but* the elephant is a very important animal here in Chanda, right?"

"If you say so, sir."

"It seems to me, Sergeant, that we can hardly expect to do anything in this place until we show the slopeheads we understand their country. That's been my big problem here, see? Now I have a plan to change this, and I want to put you in charge of it. I'm willing to forgive and forget. What the hell, every man needs some liberty."

Pause again. Campo filled it up with "Yes sir."

"I want to implement this right away. We've got a big inspection coming up, and I don't mind telling you that I plan to have us ready, Top."

Maybe, just maybe you shouldn't have told me that, Campo said to himself; because now I know you didn't file me out of here in your Unit Diary, because you don't want any embarrassments there on the paper; so maybe, just maybe, I'll bargain after I hear your terms.

"Now the way I see it is we need an elephant."

Campo nodded, expecting the Colonel to go on. There was a long silence.

The Colonel cleared his throat. "Where would we get an elephant, Sergeant?"

"I don't know, sir. I just got here."

"Well, it seems to me that has to be our first step. See what you can do about that. Shouldn't be too much of a problem for a man of your training and initiative."

The Colonel laughed and Campo knew he was free and off the AWOL charge. "I'll try to get us one, Colonel," said Campo in that Senior NCO tone that gathers the hymns of slaves and orations of anarchists into the same pitch and voice.

"Now I've been doing some reading on this, Sergeant, and we need—" he pulled out a small notebook and leafed through it "—we need a keddah, a howdah, and a charjama."

Campo's mouth dropped open. "Sir?"

"A keddah, a howdah, and a charjama. You know what those are?"

"No sir."

"Neither do I, but I'll find out."

"Yes sir."

"Any questions, Sergeant?"

No more than a billion, thought Campo, but he waited until the jokes were in the back of his head again and he acted serious. "I was wondering what we were going to do with the elephant once we get it. If that's not moving too far ahead, sir."

"Not at all, not at all, Top. Glad you asked. Well, I guess the first thing we'll do is ride it around town just to show the folks what we're all about. Ride it to work, ride it to lunch, things like that. I know there will be problems. I know that. Anything worth doing has problems, right? But if we can show the people that we understand their customs, our job will be a lot easier. And General Grider will know we're doing our best. OK?"

Campo shook his head in a confusing motion that said yes and no at the same time.

"You know, Top, here in Chanda we've got some real competition. The Russians are here, the British, the French, the North Vietnamese, the Chinese, and so on. The list is huge. And we have to look our best. As far as I know, nobody has ever thought of this idea. It'll be spectacular!" Kelly rubbed his hands. "You scout around. You snoop and poop and get me that elephant. Only one thing—don't disappear on me again, you understand? I'll write up more Charges and Specifications that you can dream of if you go U/A again. I'll string your butt from the flagpole. You better believe that."

Oh I believe it, I believe it, thought Campo. "Yes sir, Colonel," he said, and then to himself, "As long as you need me you will be okay, but may I save my own hide when the shooting starts."

Colonel Kelly stood and extended his hand. "Good to have you aboard, Top," he said in Naval terminology that he thought would please the Marine.

"Thank you, sir, it's good to serve here," replied Campo, all the time thinking of the opium den and his dreams, all the time laughing at how easy it was to lie to a Full Bird as soon as you knew there were better things in the world.

Out at Andrews Air Force Base, Walter Glover felt as if he was handling a crowd scene. General Grider had not shown up and the ETD was an hour away. And what an hour. Four A.M. Glover raced between a pay phone near the magazine counter and the staging area. Margaret sat on her suitcase and yawned. Martin Edelman toyed with his Press Badge.

"Walter," Margaret said in half-sleep, "why are you so fucking stupid?"

Walter ignored her. He was frantic. "He doesn't answer. I'm sure he's on his way. The Officer of the Day said he'd send a man over to his quarters."

Edelman looked at him with snake's eyes. They were not getting along. Glover retaliated. "I'm not working for you, you know, Martin? You know that? I have to try to get along with Little Miss Crypto here, but not you, Martin."

"What did I say, Walter?" asked Edelman. "I can't help it if the General wants me along for some good coverage. No matter what you told him. So peace, Walter, peace." He reached up and patted Glover on the shoulder. "It's too early in the day to get excited. There's no protocol at four in the morning. None. So relax. War is hell."

There comes a time, and it might as well be early, when every man needs to retaliate; that time is now, thought Glover. "Let me see your shot card, Martin."

Edelman pulled the yellow card from his wallet. "It's really none of your business."

"I'm in charge of the details side, Martin." Glover studied it and pretended to show surprise. "You need another polio booster. There are only two listed here."

Edelman looked desperately at the card.

"I can't let you on the plane until you...shoot up, you know? The dispensary is open."

"Come on. I can't lift my arm as it is. They gave us five shots yesterday."

"Sorry Martin. That's on my checklist, and the General wouldn't be happy if you didn't comply."

"You would be carrying a Western disease into their country, Martin. Like syphilis into the New World. Go take a needle," said Margaret.

Edelman folded his coat neatly and tucked it under his arm. "I hope someday I can repay this favor."

"OK, Martin, I've got lots to do. I can't be smoothing out the feelings of the Press at four A.M."

"Remember one thing before we even lift off, babies. After every four in the morning is a five in the afternoon. And that's when the papers hit the street. Remember that."

Edelman walked like a wounded bear towards the open door.

"You know he's right, Walter. Just because you think what you think, he's still a reporter."

"He'll write this up the way the General wants it, Margaret. And if he doesn't, his editors will. It's a setup and I don't want to talk about it. Let me see your shotcard, sweetheart."

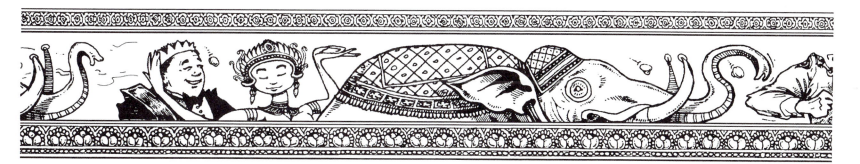

Margaret wet her forefinger and swirled it around in Walter's palm. He jerked his hand away in embarrassment. "Let me see your shotcard," he demanded, all the time looking around to see if anyone had noticed.

"Hmm hmm," Margaret whimpered in mock passion. "Let me see your needle first. I mean, I'll show you mine if you'll show me yours."

Danny Campo saw his life as a series of absurdities brought on by Commanding Officers. As he walked the streets of Royal City and tried to decide how to find an elephant, he thought back on the missions in his career that could match this one. Once in Hawaii he had been asked to bargain for one hundred pairs of snowshoes; his Company Commander was convinced that the Brigade would be sent on Cold Weather Operations. That ghosthunt failed when the men refused to contribute to the Snowshoe Fund. Then there was the American Admiral in Hanoi who used Campo's services as bodyguard (this immediately after Dien Bien Phu) rarely, but who wanted two canteens of water mixed with Coca-Cola at his bedside every morning precisely at sunrise; that hour computed by a chart the Admiral always carried. Now Campo was back on Asian territory, he had assumed possibly to die there, only to find himself wandering around like a zoo-keeper from Brooklyn, searching for an elephant.

Maybe I should put an ad in the paper if they have a paper, thought Campo.

— WANTED —

One Elephant (No tendency towards must) to work part-time American Mission House; should be housebroken; Pay Scale and Grading to be arranged; all interested apply Colonel Kelly, Field Advisor.

Yes sir, that would do it. If there was a paper, that is, and if elephants could read, and if if if.

Danny Campo stood in the center of Royal City's busiest intersection. He was at an impasse. The pedicabs swirled around him and the few taxis honked their horns at the sight of him. Campo shook his head. No, he didn't want a ride; no, he didn't want to buy chewing gum; your sister? No thanks; but if you've got an elephant? Yes, you have no elephants. OK OK.

The jumble of sheet-metal roofs and palm fronds and bamboo frames hurt his eyes. This place could get busy, he thought. The Constellation Hotel, three stories high, looked like a skyscraper. As always when the confusion of a situation tumbled his equilibrium, Campo decided to drink.

In the dark and dusty bar just off the terrace, Campo ordered a beer from Andreas. His eyes adjusted to the shadows and he saw Andreas nursing a split lip. The Greek anticipated him: "Please do not mention this to me, Sergeant." So Campo nodded and drank his beer. Andreas applied wet cloths to the corner of his mouth.

After two beers and much silence Campo cleared his throat. "Say Andreas, you know where I could get hold of an elephant? Andreas?"

"There is no market for them these days. I suggest you think of something else."

"No, no. I want a live elephant."

Andreas shook his head as he looked at himself in a pocket mirror. "My lip will not be fit to kiss for a week."

Campo shut up and drank another beer. In mid-swallow on last draining he choked as he felt a sharp slap on the back. "Mennan's the name, you old Gyrene, and welcome to this booby hatch." Campo saw one of his own heft with a cowboy hat pushed back on the neck and one puffed eye that crinkled as if it was smiling.

"Have a beer," Campo said.

"Sheeeit," spat Mennan, "and fill the bank for that bastard? He gave me this and I gave him that fat lip and that's even trade. That don't mean I have to drink his liquor. Him and that Russian go for gang-bangs, don't you Andreas? Yes sir, hit 'em and go get 'em and slide both ways. Don't do your drinking here, Top, because nobody knows what kind of saliva that mother has. Come on, I got me a good place to drink."

With his arm securely around Campo's shoulder, Mennan led him out across the terrace and into the street. As they faded into the afternoon Andreas spit once on the floor. Then he finished the open beer.

Marya Pleisetskya stared at Nadolsky. "An elephant?"

"Yes," he said as she put the phone on the hook. "Now what would they want with that?"

"It is perhaps a secret weapon. I don't know. We must cable."

"Marya..." But he did not go on. There was no use in arguing. She was independent, almost uncontrollable, and her superiors were not his.

"Alexander, you have been out here too long. You have no taste for detail. The heat has turned you into a Turk."

Nadolsky wiped his face with his red handkerchief. The woman had power. She was beautiful, but she had power. And who was he to say she was wrong?

He had recognized in himself of late a terrible and frightening desire to live in this jungle for the rest of his life. His requests for transfer, his increasing eccentricities (how could he have fallen in with the scheme of Andreas? How could he want to rape a deaf-mute? He felt a surge in his crotch and knew why), his constant bitching

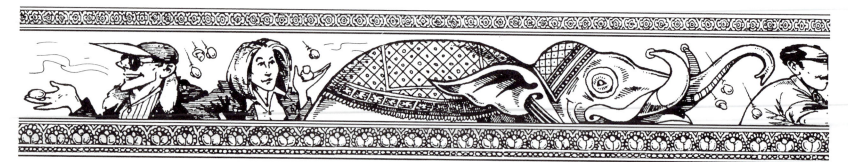

about all things tropical had been protests against his new nature. Nadolsky was appalled at what he had become, yet helpless. The icicles planted in his mind by the climate of his youth had been melted forever by this Kingdom.

And yet there was this fresh arrival, Marya the Determined, who kept constant check and totalled up his weaknesses and mistakes (so many; he had become so human) and sent these totals in reports back to Moscow. Well, give the girl time out here and she would understand. But it was a question of timing. Would the subtle vibrations of Chanda jar her frozen attitudes before he was recalled?

Recall came swiftly. He knew more than one of his kind who had been carried onto airplanes while strapped on stretchers, their bodies (corpses?) swathed in bandages, local officials protesting ineffectively. Recall.

"In India," Marya said seriously, "they are using elephants to distribute birth control propaganda. Perhaps the Americans hope to do the same thing."

To her surprise, Nadolsky leaned back in his chair and laughed loudly, longly. "What is so funny?" she asked. He shook his head as if she would never understand. "Well!" she said in a huff and left the room.

Nadolsky stopped laughing. There. He had done it again. He had set her off-balance. He had an idea that these incidents went immediately into her communiqués, all worded to prove that anything extraordinary is subversive. And it probably is, he thought, and laughed again: bless it, it probably is.

Seated backwards in the MATS Transport, Walter Glover saw the Pacific Ocean as unbridgeable and limitless. At thirty thousand feet, the water looked dull grey. Coming into Hawaii and then into Wake Island, the water had taken on that turquoise color he loved. But up high there was nothing to see, not even clouds to dodge.

Almost everyone slept. Even General Grider was sprawled across three seats, his mouth open, his snore inaudible over the whine of the engines. Glover felt his own mouth drying up as the air-nozzle sprayed old air onto his face.

Time had been fragmented. They would soon pass the Date Line. It did not make sense to his eyes to feel so sleepy. The interior of the plane was filled with bright moving shadows as if they were proceeding under the sea in a portholed submarine.

Glover read his checklist for the thousandth time. He was nothing more than an errand boy on this trip. His Introductory Report had been treated with administrative contempt. It was not even distributed. Nor, probably, did it need to be. Each member of the Inspection Team was an expert in his own area. Hollins knew more about mineral deposits in Asia than any two other topographers. Jacobs, the fat Air Force Colonel, was a good photo interp man. The list went on. They were efficient men, specialists at their jobs, uninterested in the totality of anything. So Glover's little synopsis of Southeast Asia and its problems was ignored by all but the mimeograph machine.

In secret, Glover considered himself too mild and afraid and intuitive for this line of work. He was not made for battle over conference tables. He was filled with questions, not answers, and when his feeble probing met the prefabricated structures that the military had eternally at their command, he lost. It was that simple: he lost.

There was no debating with the military mind. Apart from its vigor and righteousness, which were frightening enough, Glover thought, there was the problem of homework, of situations already predicted and confronted and analyzed (never mind how well), decisions made and memorized, charts drawn up in explanation.

"You try it sometime," Walter said to the empty seat in front of him, "and the minute you show some doubt in your own position, zap, baby, zap, they move in and mop you up. It's like a drop of water trying to push through a wall of oil."

He saw the world as zoo or circus, and he would have laughed, but there was some kind of sadness everywhere he looked. The inevitable military commitment had already been made and this useless trip to certify and seal the process involved *life*.

"You know," he said to the seat again, "that's the last thing in the world that has no price at all. And if something is priceless, that doesn't mean it's expensive. It means it's not worth considering. It's no thing. No thing."

Glover put his head back and tried to tilt his seat even more. No soap.

The plane pushed against the jetstream and Walter slept, dreaming terrifying dreams of zoos and circuses, not as a cartoon-maker might portray them, but as a child might see most things there as ready to kill him.

Night comes early and lasts long in Chanda. Late afternoon is a time for last preparations before the fog and darkness sock into the land. Up in the dusk, Mennan sideslipped the small plane and Campo felt his guts tug.

Mennan sang into the mike and Campo winced:

It's a long way to Sayaboury
It's a long long way from home.

In the slanting sun, the hills took on tinges of blue. Seen from the air, the earth looked like a green ash heap, smouldering in spots where the tribes had slashed and burned the fields to clear them for themselves. Trails ran straight up to villages on the hilltops. The valleys were filled with shadows and mist.

Campo wondered how Mennan navigated the craft. They were flying over a moon surface with no landmarks to speak of, and after they stopped following the river Campo had lost himself completely. "What happens if the motor cuts out on you?" he asked just to keep talking in the haze.

"Well, now," said Mennan, "let's see about that," and he cut the power down to near nothing.

"What hey?" Campo said, scared. No noise except the putt putt putt of the dying contraption. Wind whistle and a slow prop. The plane drifted like a glider. Campo longed to hear the engine. Mennan cackled at his discomfort and then turned his wrist and brought the bird back to life.

"It's just over that saddle on the horizon," said Mennan.

They were headed towards Sayaboury, the village that was the center of elephant training in Chanda. Here, Mennan promised, they could order themselves a super-duper elephant that would be just right for Colonel Kelly's plan.

Besides, Campo had logged no airtime with Mennan, a fact that Mennan considered an insult. All his buddies were supposed to fly with him. It was a testimony to friendship, in his opinion, and he expected gratitude from those he waltzed through the air, those who were looped and curled and spun until the brown bag tucked over the radio receiver had been used and the victim was left gasping in his shoulder harness, his parachute heavy on his back. One of those manly christenings that demanded blood and vomit.

When they were out of sight of Royal City, Campo had been taken through the ritual. Now, after an hour's airtime, they aimed for the spot on the red horizon.

"I heard they were having a little buildup somewhere around here," said Mennan. He tilted the plane again and looked idly over his left shoulder.

When up ahead, as if they had been placed there for decoration, two little puffs of smoke exploded on the flight path. "Shit," said Mennan without emotion, and he took the plane into a steep dive. Campo wanted to say Climb, you bastard, climb! because the valley floor was coming up hard and the plane was already below the shadow line. Mennan pulled it out after Campo had fainted briefly. They flew along the treetops, belly-hopping over the contours.

Mennan explained what he was doing in the fatherly tones a dentist uses with a patient. "Ceiling on this thing is only ten thousand. They can reach that easy as you can pull a tit. So when they fucky-fuck with us, we got to go for the floor. I say we head back to Royal City right now and forget those elephants. Ain't no beast worthy flying through that crap for. I'll fly a spotter mission over here tomorrow with some on call aircraft. And if they shoot at me again, they'll buy the farm, I promise you, they'll catch hell in a basket."

"Who is 'they?'" Campo said into the mouth-mike.

"How the hell do I know who they are? Somebody down there don't like us, though. And they got flak to prove it. Listen, two years ago we didn't have to worry about that stuff. We got enough troubles hitting the landing strips and fighting the fog. So you ask me who 'they' is and I got only one answer: 'they' is anybody who makes my job tougher and my ass tighter. OK?"

"Roger OK sure," said Campo fast.

"You'd think they'd let a little old Texas boy fly his toy around without shooting at him. My, my, I am starting to earn my money now."

"Serves you right," said Campo, and he thought of the rumors he had heard that pilots like Mennan pulled in three thousand bucks a month.

"Uh-uh," said Mennan, "my Daddy always told me that when somebody says 'Serves you right' you should reach for your wallet. Because your right ain't my right."

"Bullshit," said Campo. He was ready for a drink and he wished Mennan would fly a little higher.

"Settle back, Top, we got some low night flying to do. And remember what I said; if you shit in your britches you got to clean it up yourself. Understand? It'll be your job. I won't ask a slopehead grease monkey to wash the deck off. I got principles over here, whether you know it or not."

"Ah yes, assassinations aren't what they used to be, you know. Delightful at first, just the emotional shock to titillate us all; wake up and find the telly blasting away with pictures and replays. Sumner-Clark looked to Coakley for some reaction but he was not listening. "You might as well relax. There's nothing you can do now. They are somewhere over the skyline. I don't suppose anything is on time here in Chanda, is it? Not even American Generals." Sumner-Clark smoked. "Besides, they're not coming here to see you. It's another kind of probe."

"They'll want to see my files," said Coakley softly.

"Excellent! I think we made some peachy files. And if you'll screw up your bravado a bit, they'll never know the difference. I gave you some of our best material, love, so be grateful."

The two stood in the shade of the Communications Shack. The day was cloudy and hot. Their light suits showed sweat at the armpits. At least they were not standing on the concrete griddle waiting for the plane to land.

Sumner-Clark went on filling the air with monologues to keep Coakley amused and, he hoped, a little less mournful. Coakley was such a child at times, assuming that a man like General Grider was interested in the slips and slides of an erratic and not very powerful clerk. "Nations need orgasms too, don't they? Of course they do. Something a bit more exciting than normal to give the system a delicious jolt. A plucking of national strings. You see, I have this theory—listen to me now!"

"Where the hell are they?"

"Slowly, slowly, my cabbage. They don't dare appear until Major Poon has his Band ready."

Out on the tarmac, the Major was trying to align the Royal Chanda Orchestra. They did not seem to know where to stand.

"Now listen to me," Sumner-Clark said. "I want to tell you my theory."

"I don't give a damn about your theory. I want to get this Inspection over with and get them the hell out of here and go back to the way things were. If they would just leave us alone."

"My theory is that soon assassination simply will not be enough for us. We'll need more excitement. Take the last one. I heard about it on BBC right here in Royal City. What did I say? It doesn't matter. But what did you say? What did the poor housewife say? What did all of you *feel?* I submit that if you had a National Blood Pressure Monitor at the moment people heard the news, you would have found virtually no response. No orgasm. Therefore, we are left with an inevitability." Sumner-Clark paused to see if he was in control of his nervous listener.

"Which is?" Coakley asked without interest.

"It's quite obvious, isn't it? Surely you and I know that. What happens when a thing, any *thing*, ceases to please us? We go on to the next step." Coakley snorted at him. "My dear boy, put away your whips before you feel so virtuous. Because the next step for this poor old impotent world is just ahead. We should acknowledge that, love. A progression of sensations. you know what I mean. You know."

In the deep silver stacked clouds there was a flickering glint shining like tinfoil. "That's them!" Coakley shouted.

Sumner-Clark set his spine against the corner of the shack. He wanted to feel the warm metal edge run from his shoulderblades down to the crease in his ass. Ah, that feels different, he thought when he had it all arranged properly.

Coakley wanted to go closer in order to be part of the Reception Committee. "I'll stay here for a while," said Sumner-Clark. "After all, he's not my General."

As the DC-3 landed and rolled towards the Loading Area, Major Poon made his last frantic preparations. The wind did not help, kicking up as it did and rocking the small table and microphone.

Colonel Kelly stood rigid as a post and watched the approaching plane as if he expected it to explode or disappear or run over him. Lieutenant Goodfellow was equally hypertense. Sergeant Campo tried to be, too, but without a uniform he could not put all his energies into this kind of thing.

Harry Mennan ran toward the center strip and began a majestic series of hand signals to the pilot of the DC-3. He coaxed it across the narrow metal plates that connected the Loading Area with the runway.

Behind the high grate fence that defined the edge of the airport, a number of children and samlo drivers watched the ceremony. None of them smiled or waved.

From time to time, Colonel Kelly glanced nervously at the machinations of Major Poon. He had not expected the Major to be interested or active in this supposedly Secret Tour. Yet on arrival at the airport, the Colonel had seen the Band, the table with its silver cups and old coins and bananas. Flowers decorated the corners. Rice had been sprinkled all over the place.

"What is this shit?" the Colonel had asked the Major.

"Colonel, I am in charge of the peace-keeping force, and I have decided that there will be no warlike visits to Chanda without the Kingdom presenting its own welcome." And the little man had turned away from the Colonel's sputtering arguments.

So as the ramp was wheeled to the plane and the door was unsealed, and as the Colonel and his two aides snapped to attention, the Royal Chanda Orchestra (two trumpets, two bass drums, one khene pipe) struck up, in their fashion, the completely inappropriate "Hail to the Chief." To Colonel Kelly's horror, the King appeared in his limousine, Wampoom at his side. The King carried a great garland of palm berries to the foot of the ramp and Wampoom sang into the mike:

Hail to American Chief

Hail to American Chief

Welcome to Chanda the people always happy

Welcome to City where all time flowers grow

You Number One oh Hancho General Grider

Number Ten is sure the day you got to go.

The music died away in the humidity. The General was paralyzed in anger at the publicity. The King smiled and waited. The Colonel was terrified by the whole mess and for a few seconds no one moved. Dead silence. Then Major Poon began to applaud. He turned in small circles like a bullfighter and clapped his hands rapidly, politely. The sound came hollow and sharp over the wind and into the microphone. The Royal Chanda Orchestra clapped. So did Coakley, who stood in their rear.

Soon everyone was clapping, even the General as he stepped down the ramp, and the King after he had thrown the garland around the General's shoulders, and Wampoom, and finally Colonel Kelly. Each member of the Inspection Team was applauded as the plane emptied.

Then came another pause in the improvisation. More uneasy grinning silence. Walter Glover whispered something to the General, who went towards the microphone and said, quite gruffly while he was clearing his throat, "It's nice to be here." The General's dark suit was rumpled and he tugged at the center vent. "Thank you," he added. The loudspeaker screeched. Martin Edelman wrote rapidly on his scratch pad.

The day darkened. The clouds moved fast. A wall of rain and fog rolled towards the airport. In this no-man's-land of new protocol there seemed to be no one who could take charge and break the group out of its formation. It was as if they had come to a bad party and it was too early to leave. Silence again while all wondered what to do.

When from across the way behind the airport fence came the strange sound of wolf howls: Aieee, aieee, came the high falsetto. Sumner-Clark pushed his back away from the shack and scanned the fenceline. Aieee again. The group around the plane began to look too. But Sumner-Clark was closest to the crowd, and he saw them first, although he did not understand what he was seeing. For there in the midst of the little people stood a tall black man with his closed fists raised in the air, the knuckles touching the barbed wire that crowned the grating. Making no sense to those who watched him from the tarmac, Charlie Dog cried out his angry howls. As if that was not spectacle enough, Sumner-Clark's vision settled on the tall dark woman at the black man's side. Draped in a sari of pheasant colors, she too had raised her hands and was shaking them. Her fingers formed the V sign. Truly she was the more frightening of the two for Sumner-Clark. Her mouth was wide open and her head shook but there was no sound from her, no sound at all try as hard as she might, and Sumner-Clark thought for a moment that she was strangling on her own tongue.

The rains came.

"Tell me some more about them *phi*, Buon Kong," said Charlie Dog. He had been drenched and his clothes were drying on an upper bunk while Dawn rubbed his skin with coconut oil. "Tell me about the way the *phi* can help us."

"The *phi* are very disobedient," said Buon Kong. "And they help the disobedient."

"Hey, that's OK, Buon Kong. That's **bo penhang**."

"The *phi* are those spirits in us that seek liberty."

"I got mucho *phi* in me, then, Buon Kong."

The old man nodded through the smoke. "All men are born disobedient. They must be forced to work, to fight, to respect leaders. They are twisted out of harmony."

Charlie Dog sat up. "That may be, but I don't see the world changing, no sir. Trouble with the *phi* is they can't do anything, you know?"

"Perhaps," said Buon Kong. "But perhaps if we are ready to accept them, they can do things."

"I don't know, man. You talk about these here *phoo* love-ins and stuff. Maybe, I don't know."

"I will tell you a story," said Buon Kong. "Once upon a time, when Yak was King of Chanda, there was nothing but war. The people were tired of war, but Yak always said war was necessary for them. No one could break through his arguments because no one else had his means of knowing things. If Yak said the country was being attacked, how could the people debate this? He rarely came to the marketplace himself. His ministers were able to make up convenient reports. How could the people know what to do?

"But one day Yak did come to the market. Too many people had been protesting his remoteness and he wished to pacify them. 'I am here to answer your questions,' said Yak.

"There were many questions from the crowd, but they were not disobedient questions, for Yak chose those who would be permitted to ask things of him in public.

"Then a voice asked, 'Do you eat rice, oh King?' Yak smiled and said that he did. A vendor came forward. He held one small grain of rice between his thumb and forefinger. 'This is for you, oh King,' the vendor said. The crowd laughed uneasily. They were not sure if this was insult or ignorance operating. 'Please eat my rice,' said the vendor.

Yak raised the grain to his lips in a sporting fashion. The vendor grabbed his wrist. 'But first I must warn you that my rice is grown by the *phi*, oh King.'

"Yak stiffened and the people gasped. The vendor went on. 'Each grain represents the hide of one buffalo. The harmonious man eats my rice and licks his lips and says, 'My, what good rice.' But the man out of harmony eats just one grain of rice and the buffalo hide swells to its full size. That man is immediately marked for life with a stomach as large as a pregnant woman's. So eat my rice, oh King, and let us see what you are.'"

Buon Kong puffed on his pipe and was silent.

"Well come on, Buon Kong," said Charlie Dog, "what happened? Did he eat the rice?"

"Of course not. He handed it back, saying that there were too many hungry people in his country to waste rice on the leaders who were well-fed."

"So that pissed the people in the marketplace, didn't it? They wanted to see the King take the test?"

"Perhaps. But the Ministers and others in the crowd cheered the King and many people followed their gestures."

"But the King was all shook up and things like that and there wasn't no more war while he was King, huh, Buon Kong?"

"Oh no, there were many more wars while Yak was King."

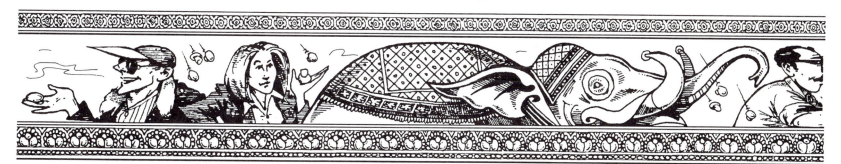

"What's the fucking point, Buon Kong?" asked Charlie Dog in exasperation. "I thought you were all for the *phi*, but I don't see what you got to prove with this story."

The old man handed his pipe to Dawn and stretched out on his pallet. "Well," he sighed, "I am sorry too, but sometimes my stories don't turn out the way I want them to. Anyway, Charlie Dog, think about it. It could happen."

"Yeah," said Charlie Dog as he lay down for another massage, "yeah it could. About the time I turn white and rich, Buon Kong. Right about then."

Buon Kong spoke very slowly in his near-sleep. "We will need the *phi*, so please do not disown them. This city is filling up with unharmonious spirits, and we must leave here soon."

"I'm for that, baby. This town is so fortified it looks like they're going to hold the next Convention here." Charlie Dog relaxed as Dawn kneaded his shoulders.

"And speaking of that, who's the Mayor of this place, you know, Buon Kong?"

The old man was asleep.

"I think airplanes make me horny," said Margaret. "You suppose so? The vibration, maybe. Or the cabin pressure. I'll bet that's it, huh, Walter?"

They were lying under mosquito netting in the musty hotel room. It was late in the evening, and Walter assumed that everyone had been channeled to the proper room by Andreas.

The first preliminary meetings had been held. It was time for sleep now. The General was a stickler for programmed rest periods after long flights. This was fine with Walter; it gave him more time for humping.

"This is a nice little country, you know, Walter? It's kind of cute. We should get out and look around."

"OK. We'll take a picnic."

"Hey yeah. With a wicker basket and lots of coconuts and things."

"Sure. We'll just tell the General that war is hell and we have to take a break after our break."

Margaret sulked at his sarcasm and pulled the cotton coverlet over her breasts. Walter pulled it down again and kissed them.

They drank a banana liqueur, the two diplomatic staffers in white cotton karate uniforms that symbolized High Tropical Camp to their tired minds.

"You look like a ghost in that light," said Sumner-Clark. He turned down the lantern until it glowed orange.

"I feel like a ghost."

"What did you learn in school today?"

"They're bringing in some kind of Task Force," said Coakley.

"I know that. They want us to put in a detachment or two with you. Hands across the sea and all that. The question is, when and where will the Task Force be sent."

"Yes, well I talked to Glover about that. Not that we're supposed to know anything or discuss it with you, for God's sake. He's not such a bad man, that Walter. I used to think he was a Puritan."

"But for a Statesider he understands a lot?"

"Exactly."

They sat on the rickety balcony and watched the river far down the slope. The bats crossed through the moonlight like bullets.

"When and where?" Sumner-Clark mused after a long silence.

"It seems to me," said Coakley flirtatiously, "that I spend a great deal of time writing your reports."

Sumner-Clark feigned injury. "You are speaking to the man who saved your starred little ass from the embarrassment of empty filing cabinets."

"So I am. And so I tell you that *when* is almost immediately and *where* still has to be determined." They pondered this in the dark.

"They'd better not decide to sit at the airport if they come in here. They'll have to move around."

"Glover and I are arguing for the river; just come up to the other side of the river so they're not in Chanda proper. But Grider keeps pulling out these air recon maps that I've never seen before and he keeps screaming buildup.

Sumner-Clark yawned. "Almost bedtime. Sleep on a powderkeg. Don't sneeze, don't cough, don't wake the animals." He stood and stretched and rubbed the back of Coakley's neck. "If those big meanies come in here and tear up my sandbox, I'm leaving. I'll tell you that."

"Leaving for where?"

"I don't know exactly. But I mean it. I've been changed here, and I like it, and I won't play war games with them."

"That would be the end of your career," said Coakley. "Think carefully about that."

"End a career—begin a life. That's what I say."

Each laughed a quiet laugh. They went inside. The bats crossed through the moonlight like bullets.

The basement floor of the Constellation Hotel was covered with rat droppings and broken glass and sand. Andreas put the vodka bottle down and hovered over the switchboard. Actually, he was trying to look down Marya Pleisetskya's cleavage. In the heat, she had taken off all but her bra and skirt. She hardly noticed Andreas. He poured her a drink. No reaction. He waved it under her nose. She ripped the earphones off her head and scolded him.

"Andreas, how am I to listen if you are always interrupting me?"

"Please drink this, Marya. It is late and you have two more hours before Nadolsky takes over."

She sipped from the cold tumbler while she held one earphone in her hand. "Are you sure this was wired properly, Andreas? I am picking up very little conversation."

He checked the switches and flipped a few. She shook her head. "Nothing."

"That should be the General's room."

"He snores."

"Perhaps he will talk in his sleep."

"I do not think this is very efficient," she said.

"I am sorry, Marya Pleisetskya, but how could I, a poor Greek—"

"Shhh! I think I hear something." He had flipped another switch and she listened very intently. "Who is in this room, please?"

Andreas checked the board. "Walter Glover."

"No one else?"

"No, not listed."

She held her pencil poised over her notepad. She pushed the earphones tight against her ears. Andreas smiled and waited to watch her copy. Nothing. He tapped her on the shoulder.

"*Shhh!*" she said. "Go away!"

"What secrets are you learning, Marya?"

She did not move except to cross her legs. "Shhh!" Her face grew red. Then she remembered that she was supposed to be transcribing and she made a few ineffectual marks on the paper. She squirmed. Andreas made as if he would flip the switch and she slapped his hand. He laughed.

"I too would like to hear these affairs of state, Marya."

Embarrassed, she handed him the earphones. He listened for a time, then shared them with her, each holding one earpiece. Andreas pulled her gently away from the switchboard.

"What are you doing, Andreas?"

"I think we should also make some policy," he laughed.

Marya smoothed her hair in a prim gesture and flushed red again. "This is a listening post. I cannot leave it."

Andreas laughed again as he led her towards the door. "If the floor was suitable I would not ask you to leave it, dear Marya. We could lie here and listen."

"Andreas!" she scolded again.

"But since the floor here is worse than the beach at Paliokastretsa, I must take you to my room. Come along, Marya."

She did not resist. But she tried to admonish him even as they reached his bed. "You must hurry, Andreas, for my watch is over in two hours."

He groaned as he entered her. "You set the limit," he said, "let me set the pace."

For some reason, he was not sure why, General Grider found himself awake at two in the morning. He wished his day could begin then. There was so much to do.

The previous day had been a success. Grider had taken it upon himself to stage a training problem for his own staff and some of the Chanda Army officers. It was a short course in special tactics: How to hold and defend Royal City. No one seemed to have thought properly about that before. Colonel Kelly had grand plans and Kong Le, the little Captain, had no plans. Grider had been amazed but had tried to hide it. After all, that's what he was there for; to pick up the chunks of incompetence that were falling all about him.

So, working from maps of all scales and compass, and riding through town in a convoy of quarter-tons that raced from point to strategic point, the group had written up a scenario of a possible attack against the city.

One thing bothered Grider more than any other. Colonel Kelly had been bitching about the lethargy of the Chanda officers. But on this particular day that Grider had been able to work with them, they seemed alert and observant. Kong Le had taken notes all day, and when the time had come for a summation of what they had learned, it was Kong Le who understood the strategies they had just created.

Under the flame trees in the Mission yard, his tigersuit rumpled from a long day, the Chanda Captain had added a suggestion of his own that was good enough for Grider to want to use as his own in his report he was writing: "You say all time, General, we got to have airfield and radio station. We got to hold waterworks and power station. We got to control post office and telegraph and maybe government buildings. That way city is took over. I say OK, General. Number One plan. Also maybe one more things." Kong Le held up a small transistor radio for all to see. "We got many radios now in Chanda. Radios up yinyang. OK, we listen good. First thing you got to hold is radio station. Each soldier wears radio around neck like this—" he looped a shoelace around his neck and tied the radio to it "—tune in, get orders. Very easy. You like?" The Captain smiled nervously and scratched himself.

Grider smiled back and commended Kong Le.

Yes, Grider thought in the middle of his insomnia, given a little leadership in American know-how and these people could think for themselves. Grider sighed against his pillow: I can't be everywhere at once in this world, but Jesus I'm a smart son of a bitch sometimes; imagine how much I've done in a day.

The three of them had taken nervously at first to their bicycles, but the road leading north out of Royal City was flat and moderately paved for the first mile. After that, as the foliage thickened and the arching trees came together over the road to form speckled shade, each had recovered the childish pleasure of balancing and pedalling.

Both Glover and Edelman carried portions of the lunch that Margaret had packed for them. Edelman wore a rucksack on his back. Glover had appropriated saddlebags. Margaret hauled the thermos of cold rice wine in her handlebar basket.

It was their plan to follow the road upriver until they found a picnic spot. They were prepared for leisure after several days of conferences and pressure, and none of them tried to speed the pace or throw challenges.

The heat was not too severe. The sun was present between clouds.

They wheeled through a village, and lowland children ran after them until they passed into the jungle road again. Neither the old men nor the chickens squatting under the huts made them any gesture.

Walter gave a running lecture on what they were seeing. "They refuse to lock up their animals. The stock would die if you did, they think. It's worse up in the mountains. They let the animals sleep with them in the huts there."

When the road got too steep to ride on, they dismounted and walked toward the noise of a waterfall. Glover broke trail into a green and grassy area that looked over the river. It was a cliff, of sorts, and Margaret stayed far from the edge and spread the luncheon, while Edelman and Glover threw stones out into the air and watched them arc towards the white-capped water that curled against itself.

Back on the checkered napkin, they drank the wine and tried to name the trees. Walter pointed to a huge sandalwood across the river. "When a King dies, they have to find a sandalwood tree that has no rot at its center. It has to be big enough so that the body can sit up when it's hollowed out. That means it has to be over a century old, usually, and sometimes they have a hell of a time finding a good one."

The sun turned critical, and Glover and Edelman stripped to their undershorts and lay dazed and tired against the soft earth. They enjoyed the fashion in which Margaret waited on them and made them feel worthy of rest. They all talked of what they were learning.

"The diseases over here," said Edelman. "TB, yaws; it's unbelievable. Malaria—"

"—Three kind malaria," said Glover.

"—Liver flukes, leprosy, worms—"

"—You got three, no four kind worm, Roundeye," said Walter again in mock-Oriental manner. "You got Menu A, hookworm and strongyles. You got Menu B, roundworm and tapeworm. You also got in fortune cookie: trachoma, pellagra—" It was not funny and he stopped his routine. "There's so much to do here," he said softly.

They ate goat's cheese and bread. Margaret poured wine when it was needed. "You'd be a good neisan, you know that?" said Glover to her. "The women over here do most of the work."

"Fine and superfine," said Edelman. "Just the way it ought to be. Fix my food and draw my bath and then go out and plant a little rice for me and the kids."

"No arguments, Martin," said Margaret. "It's too nice a day. Besides, I agree with you guys. Men are weaker. I'm serious. This is the only place I've seen where they acknowledge that poor little malformed chromosome and all it means." She patted both their foreheads. "Sleep for a while, babies. I'm going to get out of this rig and and take my own sunbath." Both men raised their heads slightly and squinted at her. She laughed. "I am *not* horny and I don't want to play doctor. OK? I just want to get some sun, damn it."

She stripped and stretched out between them. The wine and the sun and the easy noise of the waterfall led them into sleep. Edelman snored and turned away on his side. Glover dozed for not long, woke excited and erect, took off his shorts and pushed his penis against Margaret's thin thigh.

"Not now, Walter," she mumbled and he said OK and continued to nestle his face in her neck and collarbone. When he was not dreaming, he could half-open his eyes and watch her breasts rise and fall with her

breathing. Her sweat was sweet to his tongue. Once a bee teased him by trying to settle on her nipples, and Glover felt amused at his own protective instincts as he stayed awake to brush it away.

"Walter, you are a good kid," Margaret murmured to him once as she turned and cupped herself inside the curve of his thighs, her buttocks resting against his mildly stiff prong.

The three of them slept.

Until Glover felt the pressure of his bladder building. He pulled himself slowly away from her so he would not wake her. He tiptoed, ludicrously, as if he was crossing a creaking floor, towards the thicket line to find a place. "I've got to pee," he kept saying to himself, and then he admonished his stiff dick, begging it to droop long enough for comfort. "Come on," he said to it, "where are you when I need you?"

It was probably his last full thought, for as his foot kicked past a vine, his toes caught on a rigid catgut fishline that was tied to a treeroot, and the line led up to the rusted ring of a grenade that was wedged in the fork of the tree he stumbled against, and the ring snapped away with a slight ping-sound that could not be heard over the water or the air, and as Walter straightened his back and looked down at his feet to see what had tripped him, the grenade passed through its delay-time and blasted off most of the right side of his head.

All day in the opium den Buon Kong had been receiving reports. Runners came, as if to Court, and whispered to him while they knelt near his seated figure. The old man listened but rarely asked a question of them.

When Charlie Dog and Dawn came back into the room from their pad, Buon Kong signalled that they were to sit with him. "The news is not good. Tonight we must leave Royal City as soon as it is dark."

"What's happening?" Charlie Dog asked.

"There will be fighting here tonight. You may stay if you wish, but I must lead those who want peace out of our City."

"I'm with you, Buon Kong," said Charlie Dog. "But where we got to go in this world? Seems like trouble comes around no matter where I am. Anyway, as soon as we cut out of here, they'll come looking for us. That's one thing the power-boys can't tolerate, Dad. Worst thing you can do to them is ignore them. And they're not about to let that happen. No sir. The one thing to get every mother and his gun out snooping for you is to drop out."

"Perhaps," said Buon Kong. "But I want to take my people to the place of the *phi*, the Plain of Elephants. It is there that we must try to survive."

"Man, that's a long walk, Buon Kong." Charlie Dog thought about that for a time. "OK, I'm with you babies, but I got to get me some pot to smoke on the way up there. That trip is so long it'll take another one to make it."

"Something's going on," said Sumner-Clark. "I can't quite place it but something's happening."

"You mean the natives are restless?" asked Coakley.

"Something very much like it. I'm sorry to sound colonial on you, but..." and the sentence faded off as he drank his mineral water. He held his glass in the air and looked at it. "The time to leave a city is when the water becomes more expensive than the wine."

Coakley picked at his food. Luncheons were often a chore where his mind would not slow down. "I don't know any more than you. The General seems busy and Kelly can't stop talking about this elephant scheme of his.

Glover is off in the woods somewhere on a picnic. I haven't seen anything that abnormal."

"I don't know, I don't know," murmured Sumner-Clark. "The Comm Shack had been frantic. Messages all over the place. But I don't care about that, really. You never learn anything that way. We're busy enough with our codes, what with that Task Force about to come in. It's not that."

"Then what is it? Are you reading coffee grounds again for your political projections?"

Sumner-Clark smiled. "In a way, I suppose I am. Little things, bits and pieces."

"For example?"

"For example, Kong Le had his whole battalion out for a rifle inspection this morning. *Early*."

"Window dressing," said Coakley. "He wants to put on a show for Grider. Probably has visions of Staff School in the Land of the Big PX."

"Yes, I want to think that too. But the inspection wasn't on the Training Schedule, was it now? And I must say that's the first time I've ever seen the Chanda Army do anything *extra*. I just don't know about it." Sumner-Clark rubbed his eyes with his knuckles. "I've been in this business too long, I guess. The details bother me now, not the big picture. Little things." He paused again and thought it out, remembering how doll-like the Chanda soldiers had appeared as they stood for inspection in the early morning fog. What part of that picture was out of place He snapped his fingers. "Their cartridge belts!"

"Are you cracking up?" kidded Coakley.

"Their cartridge belts were drooping. They were heavy. Magazines, even the BAR-men. Those little shrimps had ammo issued!"

Coakley shook his head and laughed. "It's ironic how we panic when the army we are supposedly training gets its hands on live ammunition."

"Yes, well you go ponder the ironies, dear heart, while I write up a report."

"To whom and for whom? There's not going to be any revolution, Hilary. They don't know how to go about it. By all means go and write your report if it will make you feel better. But I am tired of reports that are never read. I can see us on the last minute of the last day describing our own burning flesh, you know? Reports are cheap."

Sumner-Clark was not listening. "One other thing. *Very* strange indeed. They were passing out radios."

"Prick Tens?" asked Coakley.

"No, no, not those lovely things." Both men laughed. "Little radios. Hong Kong Specials, to everyone. Not just the radiomen. Everyone."

Coakley poo-pooed this. "Must have been a good haul on the black market. Damn it, I told Kong Le to cool that sort of thing. He thinks he's an alderman or something. One day I had to watch while he gave each man a can of hot dogs. For meritorious conduct he told me later, laughing up his snout."

"Strange," whispered Sumner-Clark to himself.

"To paraphrase a brilliant philosopher I know, you go ponder the strangeness of it while I go back to work. Grider has called meetings into the night, and he's screaming for poor Walter. 'Where is that shitbird?' he asked me as I left. 'I'm sure I wouldn't know,' I said. 'Am I the Defense Department's keeper?'"

They laughed together again, not cheaply or roguishly, but like children who genuinely enjoy each other and who have no other friends.

"Colonel," said General Grider. "I think there are more important things to worry about than elephants. Now I understand what you want to do. That's got to be your business. But we can't fund it straight out. How would that look on a requisition? I can see some Dove getting his hands on that and telling the American taxpayer we're running a zoo instead of a war over here. There are other ways of funding it, aren't there? Build up your Special Services account and chalk it off as football equipment or something. Jesus Christ, Kelly, I shouldn't have to tell you how you do that." The General slammed his fist on the desk to emphasize his irritation.

By that time, Colonel Kelly did not care. Both men were tired enough and drunk enough to drop formalities. The day's meetings had been plagued by cables from Washington that were filled with critical questions. Their preliminary suggestions for intervention in Chanda had stirred up the specialists at home who wanted to cover their own tracks in case of crisis.

Now in the evening dusk, the two men shared a fifth of bourbon and complained to each other. They did not bother to turn on the office lights, and as the sun faded, each man had the comforting feeling that he was really only talking to himself.

"It's a good fucking idea. I want to go on record as saying that." Kelly nodded at his own hands.

"So recorded. Now let's figure out where my three little lost sheep are and whether I should send out a Search Party."

"I'd say they stayed late at their picnic and will be straggling in soon."

"Not having the responsibility for them, you'd say relax, huh?"

Kelly laughed at the insinuation. "Exactly. I'd say hope for the best. I'd say don't do anything, and maybe they've been ambushed by the Bulgarian Bicycle Cops and maybe you'll lose your command for that and I'll move up one on The List."

Grider shuddered in the near-dark. He held his wrist in the air and squinted at his watch. "I'll give them another hour." He yawned. "To think we've got another meeting. I'm tired of maps. They should be like comics; they should come in other colors."

"Read right and up," said Kelly uselessly, quietly. He was almost asleep. He did not hear the knock on the door.

"Come in," bawled Grider.

Harry Mennan, hat in hand, tried to see the Colonel in the dark. Mennan seemed very hesitant. "Colonel, I came by for the envelope."

Kelly did not register.

"Me and Sergeant Campo thought we'd do a little night flying, Colonel, and we, uh..."

Kelly jumped to his feet. "Oh, the envelope, the envelope. Certainly." He rooted through his desk drawer and, after much fumbling, handed Mennan a large folder. "There you go, Harry. Give them hell."

Mennan seemed surprised for a minute and then picked up the cue. "Yes, sir. We will, sir." He smiled nervously. "Thank you, Colonel."

"See you first thing when you get back in the morning. OK?"

"Yes sir, Colonel, the very first thing," said Mennan as he ducked out the door. Then, thinking he was being friendly and suave, Mennan stuck his head back in and said, "Maybe the second thing if I got to take a crap."

He laughed loudly at his own joke, heard nothing but silence, and shut the door fast.

"What was that about?" asked Grider.

"Oh, just a little mission. Nothing at all."

Grider yawned again. He stood up and flipped the light switch and looked directly at Kelly. "Sometimes I think you know more than you tell me." There was nothing to add to that, and the General left the room to get ready for the next meeting.

And outside, on the road to the airport, Mennan drove furiously while Campo held onto the chassis of the quarter-ton with one hand and the envelope with the other.

"If you lose that little brown bitch, I'll have your ass," yelled Mennan over the noise. "That's got more money in it than I make in three paydays."

"Now I respect you," Campo shouted, "you rich fucker."

"That's private funds, Top," Mennan said righteously. Then he launched into his instructions. "Remember what I told you. Them mountain folks near the Plain ain't nobody to mess with. We don't get out of the aircraft all night. They light the strip while we land. You give them the envelope when they come up for it, and they go away and count it. We sleep if we can, and in the morning they bring a couple of tea chests over to us. We let them load, because those chests are lined with zinc and they are heavy. They got to go under your feet and you'll be cramped on the ride back. We don't check nothing or say howdy or good-by. We just haul our asses off that Plain when the fog lifts."

"I'm going to have a hard time sleeping with those monkeys all around us somewhere."

"Yeah, I know, and maybe nobody should sleep. I'll keep the canopy open so we can hear them if they start getting restless. But worry about the spider on your balls before you worry about the one across the road. First thing we got to do is land my little BirdDog on that shit-ass strip. They usually choose a briar patch for a runway, too." Mennan stopped the jeep outside the lights of the Comm Shack. "I'll sign us out. You get the chutes. Don't come in, just get in the bird."

Campo shook his head. "This may be more than I bargained for."

Mennan was truly hurt. "You're my buddy, ain't you?"

"Yeah," Campo said slowly.

"And you'll get your cut."

"Yeah!" he brightened.

Mennan sang to himself in a country whine as he walked to the shack:

When it's poppy picking time in Chanda
We'll do as all the other poppies do,
When it's poppy picking time in Chanda
I'll feather my little nest for you.

The den was crowding up and Charlie Dog got a little claustrophobic. Signals had somehow been given across the city. As he came out into the night air he saw the streets lined with people, all standing silently close to the porches and shops. Charlie Dog went back down for Dawn and brought her up to see.

"Look at that," he said to her. "I think the old guy is taking the whole town with him. Sugar, this is scary." He hugged her tight for comfort.

At the end of the street, the crowd parted. One of the King's cars nosed toward the den.

"They're going to bust us," said Charlie Dog. "That's the King."

But as the front door opened, Wampoom slid out of the car. She carried a small satchel. "She's with us, too?" Charlie Dog wondered to himself.

Like peasants with pikes at the rising of the moon, like nervous paratroopers hooking onto static lines for a night jump, the crowd picked up litters and wagons and samlos. They began to file out toward the road. A few lanterns were lighted, but for the most part they depended upon the moon and their instinct.

Buon Kong was carried along in a wicker seat. Charlie Dog noticed that he had his pipe with him. The old man did not speak as he rode between his porters. As he was transported towards the head of the column, the people moved to the shoulders of the road to let him through.

Charlie Dog felt lonely. Dawn held his hand as they walked. He wanted to talk about what they were doing and the risks they were taking. He had visions of the column being strafed from the air or ambushed on a road curve. He wondered if they could reach the Plain in a night's walk. Not all of these people would, he knew that. There were old folks and children. There were mothers marching with babies at their breasts. Dogs sniffed and trotted haphazardly around the perimeter.

"What a crew," thought Charlie Dog. "The Crew," he said to himself. He liked the name. "This is some Crew," he said out loud and laughing. "Yes it is. I'm glad to be here, OK? This is *bo penhang*! They may bust our ass, but we're still The Crew and what the hell it's home."

He picked a crying baby from its mother's back. "Come on, sweetheart, I'll carry you and let your Mommy make milk. We got a long road to Division Street."

And they walked like that for quite a while. They did not even look back until they all heard a little pop behind them that sounded like a cork out of a bottle. The sky flashed lighter. As they turned to look, there were several more tiny explosions, and from their height above the City they saw parachute flares floating like seeds in the wind over the main part of the town.

"Aww, ain't that pretty," said Charlie Dog to Dawn. He held the baby high in his arms so the child could see. "Just like the Fourth of July, honey, whether you know it or not."

The rest of the column was strangely silent while they watched the illumination. Charlie Dog wondered why, and as he was wondering, the answer came. A streak of red tracer bullets was fired into the town from the other side of the river, and white phosphorus exploded in the midst of wooden shacks and thatched huts. Within five minutes, the city was on fire in many places.

"Oh oh, they done it now," said Charlie Dog. "There's going to be some kind of wrath around here now."

The column began to move again. The baby cried, then slept. The mother offered to take the kid back, but Charlie Dog shook his head. "No ma'am, that's OK, I don't mind. We're all in this together now with no place to go except where we're going, and I guess we ought to help each other as long as we can." He trudged farther and added to himself, really, "Before this shit hits the fan and they come looking for us. It'll be like curfew in Chicago then. Just like roundup time on Blackstone when the fuzz comes down to beat up the folks that's easy. We're going to have every damn side looking for us, we are."

Dawn wanted to carry the baby. Charlie Dog handed it to her. She kissed it with silent lips.

"Before I die I'd like to make us a baby too, Dawn honey. Why don't we hitch up somehow legal-like. Our own Legal, I mean." She smiled at him without hearing him or understanding him. Charlie Dog sighed. That was the first time he had proposed to any woman and it was his luck that the one he picked was deaf and dumb and did not realize the honor. "I must be out of my skull," he said out loud.

All lanterns doused to avoid being sighted from the city the column moved up the steep climb towards the Plain of Elephants. The firefight at their backs cast its shadows on the dark jungle.

While the exodus was passing the fringes of the City's limits, Coakley and Sumner-Clark watched from their balcony.

"Now that's herd instinct," said Sumner-Clark, trying to be contemptuous about a sight that scared him. "Like rats from a ship, do you suppose?"

"I'm going with them," said Coakley suddenly.

"How can you do that?"

"There's one nice thing about being a spy, Hilary: you can do a lot of comfortable things and claim it's all in the line of duty. Besides, I think it's our job to know what they're up to. Easy, isn't it? I'm just going to walk out there and join them."

"Hold on. I'll come to." Sumner-Clark patted his karate uniform. "We have to get out of these."

"Nonsense," Coakley said. "I can think of nothing better to wear. If we're going to be refugees, let's do it with some style. Hai Karate!" and he posed with his hands extended. The two of them raced to the road to join up with the end of the column.

The first round of illumination caught Andreas in mid-stroke. He grunted in surprise and came. Marya screamed in anger and pounded her heels into his kidneys. "Wait for me," she sobbed over and over.

When he could speak again, Andreas told her to get dressed. "All these years I have known exactly what was going on and now they fool me! We must get out of here."

"I have my duty!" argued Marya.

An air-burst of high explosive clapped like thunder in their ears. The palm outside the window was chopped apart. Marya screamed again and held her ears.

"You come with me, Marya Pleisetskya. You have your duty but I have your love." Andreas pulled her down the stairs and into his small Citroën. The car coughed and jerked toward the road leading north. Marya demanded to know where they were going.

"I don't know, little rabbit, but when we get there I will give you a medal."

Margaret and Edelman had, with the help of villagers, wrapped Walter Glover's body in the table cloth and tied the bulky sausage over the back of a small pony.

As they worked their way down the steep trail, they met Buon Kong's group coming up. They were grateful for it, indeed. It had seemed that they were walking down into some kind of inferno, the city spotted with flames.

"I don't want to take Walter back there," Margaret said in deep fatigue.

They turned the pony around and joined The Crew. "Thank you," Margaret remembered to say to Edelman when he agreed to go with them.

Edelman nodded and tried to cover his nervous, almost sentimental state with the professional reporters excuse: "There's more of a story up here than down there."

He marched automatically now in his bare feet. There was a kindness in his gestures that Margaret was not aware of. Edelman always stayed on the pony's right side. It was there that Walter's half-head still bled slightly like a crushed tomato through the cloth, and the blood dripped onto Edelman's ankles and feet.

General Grider considered himself quite composed. He was relieved to be back under fire. But the risk of Nadolsky's misunderstanding of the circumstances gave him fears for the world, and as he talked on the phone, he saw himself Saviour-like. "Yes, this is General Grider, Mister Ambassador. How are you?"

"General, I protest this aggression and when my government hears of this—"

"Yes, yes, Mister Ambassador. We protest it too. It is not our idea. That's what you've got to understand. Things are temporarily out of our control. What I'm saying, Mr. Ambassador, is we're in this together. Nyet?"

"Unless your Russian is as good as my English, I suggest we speak your language, General."

Grider laughed uneasily. He moved closer to the wall as the air-conditioner was blown into the room by a close hit. "The point is, we don't have much time to argue, Mister Ambassador. I suggest we send off appropriate cables saying that we are *all* under attack. You and us both, OK? Then we should fall back to that Staging Area near the airport, OK? You and us? Understand?"

"I cannot leave my post." Nadolsky said.

"That's up to you, sir, but Kong Le will burn this place down if he has to. Those little shacks here burn like paper anyway. I say we give him the town until we get reinforcements. He can have it. And I don't like the idea of cremating myself. Do you?"

"I do not like it," said Nadolsky firmly.

"Then let's get out of here and live to fight another day."

"It is agreed, General." Nadolsky sighed. It would be nice to have company. And where was Marya?

"Good deal, Alexander. We got some things to sort out at the airport. Like it seems that most folks pulled out of here before the shooting started. Now that's a real problem, isn't it?"

"It is," affirmed Nadolsky. "A city is nothing without people."

"*We* are nothing without people, Ambassador. That's what worries me. Kong Le can have the town for awhile. What the hell, there's nothing in it. But those people, they're our bread and butter if you know what I mean."

"I do."

"OK. So one way or another we've got to get them to come back. Understand?"

"I understand," said Nadolsky. "One way or another."

When Kong Le was certain he controlled the intersections of the main streets, the powerhouse and waterworks, the telegraph and post office, he went into the small radio station studio. He prepared to give his speech. His mind was spinning with his history, his country's history, and he almost forgot that victory was not total even by the modest standards of the plan he had devised under General Grider's naive tutelage—the airport was not his, would not be. Major Poon had been loaned enough force to keep Kong Le's troops away, and the spot was too touchy now that the Americans and Russians and French and British and the Royal Court had retreated to the place. But at this moment, he was too happy to care about the potential threat out at the airport.

The engineer in the Control Room signalled and Kong Le spoke. "My people," he said. The engineer motioned that he had not spoken loudly enough. Kong Le cleared his throat and began again: "My people, tonight I have taken a step for freedom. What leads us to carry this revolution is to stop the rape of our country. For centuries we have laid open like whores to every foreign power. I am tired of that. So tonight I did something."

He paused, thinking that he should have written this out. It was getting complicated. "I am sorry that in my strike for freedom, the City has suffered, the houses are burning, and many of my people leave for the Plain of Elephants. Come back. If we work together, we win. We say to those who think they can own us—No! Your money no good. And we say to foreigners listening now at the airport and we say to the King too—Beware! Beware!"

Kong Le stared at the microphone for several moments before he drew his fingers across his throat to gesture his cutoff by the engineer. He was mad at himself. All his life he had dreamed of a moment like this when he would take his country forward to a new independence. Words, words: he wished they were as easy to handle as platoons.

In the dark streets of the town, the Chanda soldiers set up their barricades and observation posts. They went about their work quietly. They listened to the radios around their necks. As soon as Kong Le's speech was over, the familiar voice of their Executive Officer came back on the air with specific orders for each element. There was no need for shouted commands because the radios told them everything they needed to know.

And somewhere far out in the hills around the city, The Crew struggled through the climb up to the Plain of Elephants. No one heard Kong Le's words there.

And safe inside the concertina perimeter of the airport, the King and General Grider and Nadolsky and

others listened to the speech without worrying too much. The Chanda Captain had inherited a ghost town, the routes of resupply were still open, and Royal City could be retaken anytime it was decided to do so.

"We're going to stay cool and pool our resources. I'll supply the photo recon and air cover if you'll lend us a few tanks," said Grider.

"Excellent," said Nadolsky. "Consider the tanks yours. The city will be ours by dawn."

"Fuck the city," spat Grider. "We've got to psych out those people on the Plain of Elephants. They bother me one hell of a lot more than some two-bit tin soldier who thinks he's captured the Palace when all he's really got is the outhouse."

"How can I be King without my people?" asked the King in a lonely fashion.

"You've got the picture, King Six," said Colonel Kelly. "And how can we advise an army we haven't got?"

"Yes," said Nadolsky, "and how can the confrontation of the Twentieth Century be brought to conclusion in dialectical terms if we have no people to sway? It would all be quite meaningless."

They shook their heads silently in unison as if, no matter what their differences, there was a common bond between them.

The fog stayed late that morning. The chests were delivered and loaded and the tribesmen signalled that Mennan was clear to takeoff. But he gestured helplessly at the thick soup that swirled like smoke and blocked his vision. After a time, he and Campo were left to sit alone in the aircraft and wait it out. They dozed as the fog brightened but did not lift.

Campo heard something first. He wondered if he was dreaming. The sound of distant activity was picked up by his sniper's ears. He sat straight and pushed the door farther open. Quiet voices he heard, and feet sliding through grass, and a general settling all around him.

He punched Mennan on the shoulder. "Shhh!" he warned as Mennan jumped awake. "They're surrounding us. Listen!"

"Nothing we can do," said Mennan. "If I try to take off now, I'll total out. There's no way."

Campo shook the chute off his shoulders and prepared for battle. He saw a tall figure approaching the plane. Campo pushed his foot against the wingstrut and felt his heart pump. The figure wandered about unaware, but when it came close enough Campo launched himself in a flying tackle and hit the body at the knees. They fell into the thick wet grass and pummelled each other. Campo went for the throat and missed. He was up against strength. They fell apart and scrambled to their feet. Campo threw a sharp karate punch that cut only air. Then he stopped and stared at the figure who was staring at him. It was the man he had seen running into the opium den with the girl on his arm.

"What the fuck?" Charlie Dog asked in amazement.

"Same to you," said Campo. He was embarrassed.

"That the way you treat everybody?" Charlie Dog was brushing himself off. "Instead of slipping some skin you just knock them around a little first, huh? That's some way to introduce yourself. Next time you walk on by, OK, Dad?"

"I'm sorry," said Campo. "I thought you were here to pick us off."

"Pick *you* off?" Charlie Dog laughed. "I'm here to keep from being picked off. This here," he waved his arms grandly to indicate all the territory that was slowly appearing under the fog, "is going to be my new happy home. How about that?"

Campo did not understand. Charlie Dog told him what had happened. He invited Mennan to stay, along with Campo.

"We can't do that," said Mennan.

"I wouldn't want to have to go back to the airport at Royal City," said Charlie Dog. "All kinds of confusion back there."

"Well, why should we stay here?" Mennan asked. "What's here that ain't there?"

As he said this, Wampoom walked by. She was gathering sticks for firewood. Mennan whistled at her and she smiled. "Come on, flyboy, you build big fire for me?" she asked him.

"My pleasure, ma'am," said Mennan. He took off his cowboy hat and gave a Renaissance bow. He turned to Campo. "Might as well?"

"Might as well," Campo laughed.

"Tonight we're going to have us a *phoo*," said Charlie Dog. "You all come."

Campo slapped his palms. "Never did turn down a party. Thirty years in The Crotch, and I'm still a partyboy with a few more stripes than when I came in."

The Plain of Elephants:

a place of waterfalls and rice granaries   rainbows and poppy fields

    its hills are covered with elephant grass and trees

    in the morning before the mists evaporate there is the smell of jungle pine

    the streambeds are full all year

    jungle rings the prairies and grows even to the mountains that circle the saucer of green

    no snowtips on these mountains   but smoke almost always from their flat pinnacles where the hill tribes live

    there are many tribes and many villages   the people are called the Lo but their tribes have many names such as Meo and Yao and Youne and Khalom   each tribe builds its own village near its fields of corn and cabbage and poppy   after the soil is burned and the fields are cleared and many crops have grown the villagers must move to new areas where the land is virgin and rich

    no maps can track their continual dislocation

    each day is a season

    the men wear pheasant feathers in their hair and silver collars on their necks and leather leggings when they hunt in the high grass

    women who want to please the phi wear a river stone in a leather amulet that hangs between their breasts to be sacred the stone must have been given to them by their first lover   he woos with songs like this

the fish in the river
the leech in the field
ducks in the poultry-yard
you give food to all
why are you cruel to me?

"We are now in the home of river serpents and buffalo demons," Buon Kong said to The Crew. "To aid the *phi*, let us help with the crops, let us dance and please ourselves, let us build our lives around each other. Surely the *phi* will understand and protect us. Tonight we must bury the dead one who joined us on our march."

The bundled body of Walter Glover was taken downstream to be washed and prepared for the coffin.

"To die is hard, to die is painful, yet death is a feast. Time does not move from past to present to future on a line. Rather, it swings like the seasons. The dead are our children and we are theirs. If we listen to the voices of the *phi*, we will never be owned."

Many of The Crew moved into the fields to harvest the poppies, for it was that time.

the pod of the poppy is bluish-green   it is in the form of a small flat apple
the flowers of the poppy are shaped like tulips   they are beautiful to look at   whites pinks purples
but they are not pleasant to smell
the seeds of the poppy contain no opium   they are white and blue and yellow and black
they are ground into oil

before the plants grow too high they are trimmed   those shoots growing too close to each other are uprooted   their leaves are used in salads

the fields are seeded by hand   the plants are cut and picked by hand

a few days before they are ready for harvest the petals of the poppy fall and expose the pod   this is the time of constant testing when only the wisest farmer can determine exactly which night the pods should be cut   if they are cut too soon the sap is thin and falls on the ground   if they are cut too late the morphine changes to codeine

cutting the pod is an art   the incision must neither be too deep nor too shallow and it must run only three-quarters the circumference of the pod

the pods are cut in the late afternoon and evening   the sap is collected the next morning in Chanda the night of the cutting is honored

the mature plants are taller than children   no child under fourteen may help with the harvest for you must be able to breathe above the fumes

the sap is reddish-brown on the outside of the pod and it gives off fumes that can make you drowsy if you lie down in a poppyfield at harvest-time you may not get up again   babies have suffocated while on their mothers' backs

the collection of sap is made in a small copper cup carried on the belt and lined with broadleaves

once collected the sap is wrapped in banana leaves and blocked out into bricks   each family places one small brick in the center of the old field that has just been harvested   this is for the **phi**

no one may enter the field for fifteen days until the **phi** *have smoked and enjoyed the product*   *this*
they always seem to do   *the earth of the field turns brown and only seeds and shells are left*

   there is no law against opium in Chanda

The Crew split up and worked without direction. Some built windbreaks, others worked in the fields, some carried water.

It was the foreigners, men like Andreas and Edelman and Sumner-Clark, who pressed Buon Kong about the defense of the Plain. But the old man refused to give that his first consideration: "What are we to do? We have one plane, one small car, and no weapons. Let us build whatever kind of life we can here and depend upon our spirits and those of the *phi*. Here you see the poppy harvest being taken in, a burial prepared, mothers about to give birth. These are the vital things for us."

"You got to survive," Mennan called out. "That comes first."

Buon Kong smiled. "Perhaps. But that is the cry of the unharmonious, and as long as we can, we will try to avoid that. How often have we been told that we must wrap ourselves in protection before we stop to enjoy life? And how often has that advice led to destruction?"

Walter Glover's body was washed with water that had been perfumed with mint and jasmine. A small gold coin was set between his teeth. Cotton threads, each with thirty-two knots for the thirty-two souls, were wrapped about his neck and wrists and ankles. A rough cotton shroud covered him, and he was placed in a coffin. The

wood of the coffin was sealed with the resin of the pinetree. The crude box rested on the trunks of banana trees while the funeral pyre was being built. Some women remained at the coffin's side to clear away termite hills and woodbugs.

In the wide stretch of a rice-field lying bare after the harvest, The Crew built a pavilion of bamboo frame and thatched roof. Half-walls of woven reeds were wound around three sides. Gilded paper, flowers, a few photos from Walter's wallet, and drawings were tied to the walls.

Many of the pictures and sketches were realistic portrayals of people making love. Edelman asked about this but Buon Kong replied: "In Chanda life, never loses its rights."

In the late afternoon, before the night in which Walter Glover was to be cremated, Harry Mennan tried to eat from a small bowl of rice and fish sauce. His face twisted as he swallowed the pungent meal. "Goddam," he said, "that is plain awful stuff. Smell that," and he shoved the rice bowl under Danny Campo's nose. Campo smiled but did not say anything.

Mennan looked about for sympathy. No one. "This crap smells like a fertilizer truck that run over a skunk in front of a slaughterhouse in a paper-mill town. You know that?"

Margaret and Edelman and Campo all laughed with him. But they were looking at the pyre with its piles of wood and rags, the four posts ready to receive Glover's coffin in the next hour. And to frame the scene, smoke and haze from the burning fields in the background, the *brume seche*, colored the sky and made the distant thunderheads even darker.

A long day was dying and the sun sank copper.

Night comes on fast, but the dance, the *lamvong*, starts with the setting sun. Around and around the pavilion circle the young people. It is their night to celebrate life, this night of cremation. Their favor to the dead is to use their energies and their lusts in praise of life. The girls beckon and tease—Come, come—but then they break off the patterns they have been shaping in the air and on the ground with their hands and feet. The chase must not be ungraceful, and some girls force their lovers to circle after them for hours before they wander off together.

The khene pipes wail and soft drums beat.

Candles and lanterns light the shelters.

The old women roll cigarettes of hash and marijuana. They prepare quids of betel.

No one hurries.

There are dishes of boiled chicken and fish, meat and pimentos, sweet potatoes, areca and sugar-cane buds. Rice alcohol has been bottled.

As the coffin is carried to the center of the pavilion, Dawn takes a small lighted candle between the thumb and forefinger of each hand and dances around and under the box. Her arms make arcs, and tiny flames leave momentary impressions of fiery paths in the air. Charlie Dog joins her and they dance to the drum. The other dances continue.

Eventually, Charlie Dog takes Dawn by the waist and leads her away. He wants her at that moment, but before they clear the circle of light, he stumbles. He picks up the grass-hidden white slab he has tripped on and shows it to her. It is a gravestone, windwhipped and rainwashed, all but indecipherable, and he can read only the words: MORT POUR LA FRANCE.

When the moon rises orange, a string of firecrackers and small rockets are set off down by the stream. An old man opens a wicker birdcage that holds five mourning doves and as they fly first towards the light, and then away from it, he chants:

> The body is nothing once the soul has left it
> So we are told.
> The home is nothing once children leave it;
> So we would believe.
> Birds, I release you because all things must be free,
> and the body does not trap the soul but beautifies it,
> and children are guests in the house.

More rockets are fired into the air. If a rocket is a dud, there are jokes about its impotence and the impotence of its maker; while he tries time and again to light it, girls dance around him and undress him. They hand him sticks and cucumbers and other phalli.

The last rockets are used to light the funeral pyre. The blaze builds and consumes the coffin, then the entire bamboo structure of the pavilion. The crowd backs slowly away. They retreat only as far as the flames force them.

The fire is complimented for its beauty and energy. Drinks are taken. A few people point at the moon, which this night is going into eclipse.

Neither the dancing nor the loving stops until the fire has bled itself and only ashes and smoke are left in the night. While these are stirred, Buon Kong speaks:

"To die is hard, to die is painful, yet death is a feast. We celebrate the life we are trying to lead. Here on this Plain, we will take doubt as our pillow and freedom as our food.

"Up in the sky, the moon is about to die in the earth's shadow. In Chanda, this is known as the time when the frog swallows the moon.

"In the same way, perhaps, we are all about to be swallowed by the things in this life that are unharmonious; by governments and armies, by those who would tell us how to live, if it can be called living.

"Some have said that if our children grow to maturity on this Plain, they will spoil and rot. I say that we must train our children as we train elephants, with sugar-cane and songs and stories, so that they learn to know life instead of death, so that they learn to live instead of spending a lifetime preparing for death.

"If there is darkness coming upon us as there is upon the moon tonight then let us remember that no eclipse is total, and that light shines from the deepest shadows, and times may pass, but they will return again as surely as the seasons.

"If we are to be crushed by what has become the world, by the forces that may destroy us (if the *phi* cannot protect us, if we forget how to live in pleasure with each other), then our deaths will be hard, our deaths will be painful. But we will return again with our laughter and singing and loving and all those things not permitted by the unharmonious, the powerful, the judging.

"We have tried to break away. We ask only to be left alone. But perhaps this is the greatest sin, the One Unthinkable. Nothing is more frightening to those who would control us than that we ignore them. Truly, that sends rage and terror to their mangled spirits.

"Soon, sometime soon, there will be tanks coming to crush us and planes to bomb and burn us. Let us trust in ourselves and the *phi,* and see if the gentle spirits are any match for those who pursue us. It will test us fully, yes. But remember that the *phi* have been through at least one life, and they know what some people in the world do not: that life is sweet and to be valued over property or borders or faiths.

"And we say to those who are now assembling in the valley of Royal City, we say, 'You may kill us. That remains to be seen. But at least we will not be dying *for* you anymore. At least we will die with the right things in our hearts....'"

Buon Kong dropped his arms and sat back in exhaustion. His porters picked up his chair and started to move him away, but he stopped them. With quivering steps he walked towards the ashes and stared at the pyre. Then he turned and placed two fingers to his teeth. He whistled. There was a silence, and the people listened to the whistle echo down the Plain. Then, dimly, they heard a strange noise. Whistle again, noise again.

Dadumdada was trumpeted from the jungle, and in the night, the earth shook. *Dadumdada* as a herd of elephants approached the astonished Crew.

Babu led the train of elephants toward the light. He kneeled before his old keeper and Buon Kong was lifted aboard. The Crew cheered. The elephants trumpeted and raised their trunks.

"They have come to join us," said Buon Kong from his high perch as he patted Babu's head. "It was their decision."

Cheers and trumpets again.

Darkness and fog. The ashes are still stirred, as they must be for the next days, until they are one with the dust. The lovers come back towards the ash heap for warmth. They sleep.

Only Mennan hears the sound. He sits up and cocks his head. The small noise of a vacuum cleaner high in the sky. He knows what that is, he does. He shakes his fist up at nothing. Wampoom turns in her sleep and Mennan prods her. "You hear that?" he asks. She nods no. "Listen," he says. "Know what that is? I'll tell you." And he rips the blanket off them both to show the night their nakedness. Wampoom yelps and tries to pull the cover back. Mennan laughs and rattles his stiff prong at the sky. "Take a look at that when you get back to the lab, boys!" Wampoom throws the blanket over them and mounts him; she thinks he has gone crazy. As she rides him hobbyhorse style, Mennan gets bitter and scared. "They can see everything," he says, "with their special films and infrared stuff and sidecar radar; how are we going to beat that?" But her motions are giving him some ease, and they rock in tandem, and by the time he feels his release springing up from his gut and spine he has his humor back and he giggles (at the line that bounces in his head) as he comes. When it is over, he finally manages to say it: "Smile, honey," he whispers to the limp and happy woman, "you're on Candid Camera."

A jungle dawn. The night sky dying and monkeys calling. The birds get ready for heat. Smoke, river mists, low clouds on the hills. The charcoal porters walk the trails. Out of the brush comes Buon Kong riding his elephant. Tall grass falls under the slow shifting weight. Into the circle he rides, beast kneels, dismounted is Buon Kong. Not a word. He waits.

Dawn has bathed in the stream. She comes back up the hill with her hair dripping. She is naked to the waist and the water oils her skin. She faces the rising sun and combs her hair with an elephant comb and her face has the look of seeing nothing.

The ritual of a new day begins. Dawn kneels and raises her hands to the sky. Buon Kong reaches up. On each wrist he ties a string. Each string has thirty-two knots in it for the thirty-two parts of the body and the thirty-two souls. Buon Kong leads the group, saying: "Come my soul, by the path that has just been opened, by the track that has just been cleared. Come with me and bouleversez. Take your tie and hang your ghost. Come, before it's too late."

The elephants were used for the few defensive preparations Buon Kong wished to make. They hauled trees and piled them across the trails that led towards the center of the Plain. They carried buffalo skins filled with water into the camp. And at night they stood guard duty on the far perimeters, for their trumpeting calls could be heard even in the wind.

Campo had tried to convince Buon Kong that camouflage nets and punji stakes and tank traps would be necessary. He also had a mania for what he called "fields of fire"; he wanted the elephants to clear sections of jungle that grew too close to the camp. But Buon Kong would have none of it. "There are more important things to do," he claimed.

"Such as?" Campo challenged.

"You will see," said Buon Kong. The old man was very tired and Campo did not argue with him, indeed, could not, for Buon Kong was asleep again. He had taken to sleeping often, at odd times of the day.

And so it was that one dawn, before anyone was prepared for the day, there was a fearful bellowing on the southern reaches of the Plain, and Babu and several other elephants came rumbling back to the camp with their trunks high in the air. As The Crew woke and stood about in the mist, they heard the frightening sound of tanks invisible below the horizon, a sound that once heard cannot be forgotten, as if giants were dragging chains and shaking the earth.

Two jets flew low over The Crew and dropped cannisters of leaflets. The leaflets fluttered to the ground. They read:

> TO THOSE ON THE PLAIN OF ELEPHANTS
> YOU ARE LIVING IN DISPUTED TERRITORY
> YOU ARE IGNORING YOUR OWN GOVERNMENTS
> THIS CANNOT BE TOLERATED
> LEAVE THIS PLAIN WITHIN THE NEXT HOURS
> AS ANTI-PERSONNEL ACTIONS WILL BE JOINTLY UNDERTAKEN
> ..... PEACE .....

"What's that mean?" asked Charlie Dog, "'Anti-personnel actions will be jointly undertaken'?"

"That means," said Mennan, "that they will bomb the shit out of us."

"We'll see about that," said Charlie Dog. "We'll call up a few *phi* , we will."

Mennan snorted.

"Hey Buon Kong," Charlie Dog called, "we're about ready." The old man nodded. "I sure hope he lasts."

"He don't look so good," said Mennan.

"Well," said Charlie Dog. "I guess we got to start this day."

"How?" asked Mennan.

"Like every other, with pipes and love and things. Buon Kong says that's the only way the *phi* will stick around."

"I think this is crazy, you know?" said Mennan.

"Yeah, I know, but I'd rather die fucking than fighting."

"OK, Charlie Dog, it's your funeral."

"Oooo, don't say that man, it's bad luck. Besides, it's my wedding, not my funeral."

"Your what?"

"My wedding. Me and Dawn."

"You mean while the tanks are coming and the bombs are dropping, we're going to sit around and watch you get married?"

Charlie Dog laughed. "Ain't that some trip? Not really married like church and all. Just a ceremony that the *phi* will like and all. A love-sun thing."

And the day began, the girl up from the stream, the tying of strings and lighting of pipes. Charlie Dog put on a robe of silk and took Dawn to the center of the circle. "Nobody knows how this is going to turn out," said Charlie Dog, "but Dawn and me wanted you all to join us in a sort of Sunny Day Dance, and let's consecrate this whole thing here." So saying, the music began again.

All day the battle, what there was of it, raged. Planes came in low and dropped napalm, the jelly-canisters falling like fat cigars into the treetops. But the pilots found their aim off-target and their compasses and sights disturbed by strange vibrations. The tanks that roared over the feeble barricades lost their treads for no reason whatever and the elephants towed the helpless vehicles back down the trail.

When the first radio reports reached Royal City, General Grider did not believe it. He ordered more armor, more planes, with the same result.

"Magnetic field, my ass," said Grider after he interrogated one of his best pilots. "Magnetic field! That's not enough to stop a jet plane."

"They don't stop them, sir," said the pilot. "They just divert them. We can't get a straight shot. All those people out there in the middle of that prairie and we can't get to them. I made five passes before my bomb release would work, and then it was ten seconds late. Like to blew me up, General."

Nadolsky paced about the shack. "Russian tanks are Russian tanks! No one stops us! But we cannot get near the place. Do you know how long it takes to change a tank tread? And we must keep something in reserve down here. It's impossible!"

Colonel Kelly shook his head. "We've got everybody working on this. I don't understand it. Tay Vinh has been throwing eight shells a minute into that place, but they're all early air-bursts, and that doesn't hurt a thing. Colonel Gaillard set up a radio relay, but all we hear is static. I don't understand it."

Lieutenant Goodfellow cleared his throat and said with deep gloom, "If we're not careful, we're going to have a precedent here." The King and the officers stared at him. "I'm trying to be helpful, sirs."

"What do you suggest, Lieutenant?" asked General Grider.

All his young life the Lieutenant had dreamed of this moment. He cleared his throat again and pulled maps and charts from his special kit. "According to my computations, sirs, this would be the ideal time to drop the, uh..." His voice trailed off.

"The bomb," Colonel Kelly concluded for him. "We've got this figured down to a cunt-hair, gentlemen. The weather conditions are ideal—"

"—the wind is good—" the Lieutenant interrupted eagerly.

"—the terrain is receptive—" added the Colonel, not exactly sure what he meant by that, but he had read it somewhere, "and we have a StratoFort on call from Guam and he should be over us now."

All pondered. General Grider mused: "We need clearances for this sort of thing."

Lieutenant Goodfellow brightened. "We have just received clearance for this small a kilotonnage, sir." He stiffened. "I think the leaders of the world are as concerned about precedents as we are."

"If not more so," nodded Kelly in agreement.

"Of course they are," said General Grider. "This kind of thing could put them out of work, right, Nadolsky?"

The Russian nodded. "Don't forget us. It would put us out of work too."

"You got to nip precedents right in the fucking bud," shouted Colonel Kelly. "We can't let those people stay up there."

General Grider frowned. "What would happen if we simply left them alone?"

"No siree," said Kelly. "I can see it now." He used his hands to describe his vision. "Pretty soon other folks hear about this Plain of Elephants. Newspapers and TV build it up. You got resort hotels and jet flights and a big tourist boom. No sir."

"Are we in contact with the bomber yet?" asked General Grider.

"Yes sir," said Lieutenant Goodfellow. "I have them on the frequency and they are standing by. Two bombs loaded but not armed."

The General put his hands on his hips and narrowed his eyes. "Does anybody here object?"

Major Poon waved his hand in the air. "General, as head of the peace-keeping force—"

"Major Poon, there's no need to get your speech ready. I understand your position, but you can hardly be considered a full voting member of this body. Try to remember your status as an observer, Major." The little Indian bowed his head.

"Does anybody else object? Any who do, raise their hands, or... or..."

"Or forever hold their peace," added Kelly.

The General winced. "I wasn't going to say that, Colonel." Kelly shrugged. Grider changed the subject. "I assume all our elements are out of the area?"

"Are you kidding, General?" cried Kelly. "There must be a million elephants up there."

"Elements, Colonel, *elements*."

"Nobody flying up there now, sir. No sense to it."

"And my tanks are all in the ditches," said Nadolsky sadly. "It is not to be believed."

No one spoke. Colonel Kelly cleared his throat. "General, before you give the final order, I'd like to say something."

"Go ahead."

Kelly stood and looked each man in the eye. "I think we all know what's happening here today. And I think we are damned lucky to be a part of it. For years and years nobody knew when or where this would happen. Oh, there were guesses, sure, and books and movies about it." Kelly smiled slyly. "And I don't suppose that there was one of us in this business who didn't say to himself when he was stuck in some dog-post somewhere—and if Chanda isn't a dog-post then tell me what is—that there wasn't one of us who didn't say: Boy, I'd like to be around when history is made. You think about that, King old boy... Mister Ambassador. Our names are going to be inscribed in the Book of History. Think about that."

General Grider stood up again, "Colonel, I—"

"Just one more minute, General. I know you're rushed, but there's one more thing we got to do."

"My point is the B-52 can't hold forever."

Kelly waved in agreement. "I know that, General. But 'forever' is a relative word right about now. You can't just go out and make History without giving thanks. And that's what I want to do now."

Nadolsky slammed his fist into his palm. "If you are about to do what I think, need I remind you that The State—"

"C'mon, Alexander, old buddy. It won't hurt you to listen in for a minute. You might learn something." Kelly closed his eyes and raised his arms in the air. "Gentlemen, call it a message, call it a prayer, call it what you will, let's say a few words to set this thing up proper and to give thanks that we were the ones called on to do it." There was a silence broken only by the static from the radio handset. "Today we have been asked to teach the world a lesson. All our governments have come together with the knowledge that this lesson must be taught. It is a special moment, and we would ask certain things of it.

"We ask for accuracy from the bombardier. First and foremost we ask that, because if he slips his target grid by even a fingernail, it could be the end of us instead of those for whom and to whom this lesson is directed."

"I never thought of that!" whispered Goodfellow, but Kelly went "Shhhh!" through pursed lips and continued.

"Second, we ask that this lesson never have to be taught again, and that people all over the place, here and everywhere, learn that they got to behave. We can't have people running off to places like the Plain of Elephants. That's no good. Not only is it selfish and immoral, but it also makes more work for those of us who are trying to run this old world. We got enough headaches. We got enough troubles. People have just got to appreciate that and play along.

"Finally, we must remind ourselves that we are humble in our task, and that we just happened to be in the right place at the right time, and for that we are thankful." Kelly opened his eyes and stared around him. "Anybody get that on tape?"

General Grider slapped his hands together and walked to the radio. "Tell them to fire for effect when they are ready, and to keep us informed of what is happening."

Lieutenant Goodfellow repeated the order over the radio mike. He held the earphones close to his head to make sure that he caught all that was communicated from the bomber.

For several minutes nothing could be heard in the room except the mumbling of Colonel Kelly as he wrote rapidly on a pad of yellow legal paper, trying to remember exactly what he had said.

Lieutenant Goodfellow jumped. "Fifth fail-safe off... sixth fail-safe off... the Baby is armed... final approach... doors are open... altitude and azimuth steady... no signs of magnetic field... looks good for go... target in sight... fifteen seconds to release-time... ten... five, four three two one... she's off... fusetime now... misfire?" Goodfellow pivoted and twisted in his chair. "Misfire possible... standby... misfire what?... say again?... mushroom?... did I read your right? Mushrooms?" The Lieutenant seemed confused.

Colonel Kelly tried to clear things up. "That's not a misfire, Lieutenant. The blast just looks like a mushroom."

"Shut up and let him listen!" roared General Grider.

"I don't believe this," said the Lieutenant under his breath. He wrote rapidly on his clipboard. "Say all after mushroom. Roger... roger... roger... no shit?... roger, stand by." The Lieutenant wheeled about and faced his superiors. He was very pale. He bit his lips and looked at his feet. "The bomb crew requests permission to return to base."

"What the hell happened?" roared General Grider.

"I don't really understand it, sir, but they want to go back to Guam."

"Permission denied until you tell us what happened!"

"Well sir, sirs, we don't really know except there wasn't much of a blast and the bomb behaved badly, very badly for that kind of bomb." The Lieutenant shook his head as if he was scolding a child.

"God damn it Lieutenant, if there's some sort of dud they can go back and drop their other one."

"No sir, they can't."

"Don't you tell me!" screamed the General.

"What I mean sir, sirs, is that the crew chief reports the one in the bay broke open at the same time as the one they dropped did. You see, the one they dropped behaved very badly, as I said, and seemed to beak into little tiny pieces and they couldn't tell what was going on but it looked like everything was screwed up and about that time the crew chief reported that the one in the bay had cracked open too—"

The General interrupted to slow the Lieutenant down. "Easy, easy, Lieutenant, I just don't believe that. If that kind of bomb busts open in a bomb bay, there's no crew chief left to tell about it."

"Oh yes sir there is sir you can talk to him if you want and maybe you should sir—"

"Now easy, Lieutenant—"

"—well it's been a hard day sir and I don't believe any of this myself. Oh, I thought dropping the bomb would be very much different, I really did."

"Now easy," the General said again. "What was the report on the bomb they're carrying now?"

The Lieutenant blew his nose. "I really don't want to tell you that, sir. It's crazy."

"You can tell me, Lieutenant, you can tell me."

"Mushrooms," said the Lieutenant.

Colonel Kelly had enough. "What is it with you and these goddamn mushrooms, Lieutenant?" He mimicked Goodfellow's tears. "Mushrooms, mushrooms."

"That's what was in the bomb," cried the Lieutenant. "Thousands of mushrooms. The whole plane is filled with them. The bomb crew is very disturbed and they want to return to their Base."

General Grider sighed. He figured it was the end of a long career for him. "Permission granted," he said. The Lieutenant relayed the message. "Tell them not to eat any of those things!" the General added as an afterthought.

"Damn mushrooms could be poisonous!" Kelly called out.

"It's toadstools that are poisonous," said the General. "Mushrooms are just psychedelic."

"Same goddamn thing," said Kelly. "Go on, Goodfellow, tell them what we said."

No one spoke as the Lieutenant talked over the radio. Grider and Kelly shook their heads. "I don't understand it," said Kelly.

"Well, Colonel," said Grider, "they may rip my stars off, but I'll take a few defense contractors with me. There's no quality control these days."

"I just don't understand it," the Colonel said again. He looked out the window to rest his eyes and mind. Instead, he saw Major Poon's jeep with Nadolsky seated at the Indian's side racing off on the road to the Plain of Elephants. "Stop them!" the Colonel yelled to no one in particular. "Look at those bastards cutting out on us!"

General Grider could not get excited. "I don't blame that fat Russian. Think of what they'd do to him for this. Besides, I was reading an Intelligence Summary on him last night. They know the old goat pretty well. It turns out he's queer for mushrooms."

"I just don't understand it," said the Colonel. "I just don't."

On the Plain, The Crew spent most of the day cleaning and storing the mushrooms that had fallen over great areas of the plateau. Charlie Dog laughed to himself as he peeled and ate one of the more exotic exotics. He fed Dawn small nibbles too.

"We've been through something together, ain't we?" he called out to the whole group, to Andreas and Marya, Campo, Edelman and Margaret, Buon Kong, Sumner-Clark and Coakley, Mennan and Wampoom, the elephants, the boatmen and ballad singers and fish sellers and pack peddlers and children and dogs. "We've been through some kind of good lifetime today," he cheered as he hugged Dawn. "Hey, Buon Kong," he called across the grass, "tell us a story."

"Yes, yes," everyone cried, "tell us a story, Buon Kong!"

Babu kneeled to let his master down from his back, but the old man was asleep, or seemed to be.